THE LAW (IN PLAIN ENGLISH)® FOR PHOTOGRAPHERS

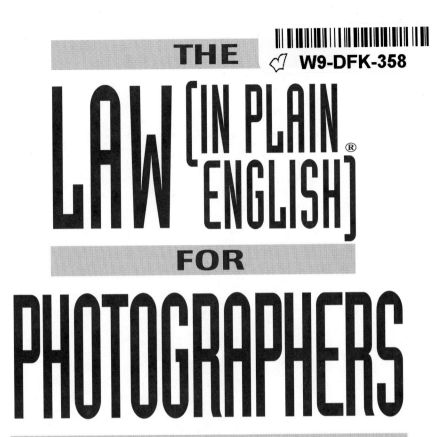

Leonard D. DuBoff

ATTORNEY-AT-LAW

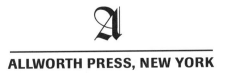

ALLWORTH PRESS, NEW YORK

Published by Allworth Press, an imprint of
Allworth Communications, Inc.
10 East 23rd Street, New York, NY 10010

Book design by Douglas Design Associates, New York, NY

Typography by Sharp Designs, Holt, MI

ISBN: 1-880559-19-6

Library of Congress Catalog Card Number: 95-075286

CONTENTS

___INTRODUCTION

I have been asked by the many photographers I represent to provide them with the name of a text which would help them understand the myriad of legal problems that are prevalent in the world of photography. Unfortunately, I have been unable to locate such a book. I therefore decided to undertake the task of creating one which would enable the professional photographer to learn about the legal problems which can and do arise in this profession. It is my hope that this, the fifth book I have written in my Plain English series, will service this purpose.

This text is not intended to be a substitute for a lawyer, rather, it is designed to educate professional photographers about potential legal pitfalls and traps so that they can be avoided. It is also designed to assist the professional photographer with legal vocabulary and concepts so that discussions with an attorney will be more efficient. Since a lawyer's time costs money, it was my goal to provide a practical, readable, and understandable volume for you, the professional photographer, so that you can either avoid legal entanglements or when necessary, seek professional assistance before a problem becomes irreparable. It is my sincere hope that this book will fulfill my expectations and your needs.

COPYRIGHT

LAW

The professional photographer is hardly likely to have a staff lawyer. So, in addition to becoming skilled at your work and getting word out to the rest of the world, you need to be aware of the potential legal problems that may be lurking in your business dealings. Once you are armed with the knowledge of what to look for, you can usually avoid potentially serious headaches.

Copyright protection is a good topic for starting this book. It is a subject about which most photographers have many questions, and it is also a legal matter that—barring infringement problems—you can usually handle yourself.

Copyright law in the United States has its foundations in the Constitution, which provides in Article I, Section 8 that Congress shall have the power "To promote the Progress of Science and the useful Arts, by securing for limited Times to Authors and Inventors the exclusive Right to their respective

Writings and Discoveries." The first Congress exercised this power and enacted a copyright law, which has been periodically revised by later Congresses.

The Copyright Act of 1909 expressly provides for the registration of photographs. Furthermore, photography has been adjudicated by the courts as being eligible for copyright protection because photography is a form of creative expression and each photograph involves artistic choices. According to the United States Supreme Court, a photograph "must be deemed a work of art and its maker an author, inventor or designer of it, within the meaning and protection of the copyright statute."

The Copyright Act remained in effect nearly three quarters of a century despite periodic complaints that it no longer reflected contemporary technology. At the time the 1909 act was passed, the printing press was still the primary means of disseminating information. But new technology such as improved printing processes, radio, television, videotape, computer software, and microfilm created the need for a revision that would provide specific statutory copyright protection for newer information systems.

The 1909 act was substantially revised in 1976. The Copyright Revision Act of 1976 became effective on January 1, 1978, and covers works created or published on or after that date. The creation of copyright in all works published prior to January 1, 1978 is governed by the 1909 act. Rights other than creation, such as duration of copyright, infringement penalties, and infringement remedies are governed by the new law. It is important to be aware of the basic differences in the two laws, and of which law applies to a given work.

The 1976 act was a product of compromise. Many of the clauses of the act were drafted to appease competing special-interest groups. As a result, much of the language is ambiguous. In time these ambiguities should be clarified by the courts, but for now some parts of the copyright law remain a guessing game. In 1988 Congress once again amended the statute so that the United States could become a party to the Berne Convention, an international copyright treaty. For the first time in the history of American copyright law, a copyright notice is no longer required; although, as discussed later, it should be used whenever possible.

Clearly, you as a photographer need to know what protection you have under the present law, and the information in this chapter should be pertinent to you. However, if you sell photographs to advertisers or publishers, they may take care of the details of copyright notice, deposit, and registration, so you may not need to concern yourself about dealing with the Copyright Office. Check your contract, of course, to make sure that the copyright is to be in your name.

Federal Preemption of State Copyright Law

One of the problems with the 1909 act was that it was not the exclusive source of copyright law. Copyright protection or its equivalent was also provided by common law (that body of law developed by the courts independent of statutes) and various state laws. This caused considerable confusion since securing copyright protection or avoiding copyright infringement required careful examination of a variety of different laws, there being no single law that covered all cases.

The 1976 act largely resolved this problem by preempting and nullifying all other copyright law—in other words, it is now the only legislation generally governing copyright protection. The act does not, however, preempt the common law or the statutes of any state for copyright claims arising prior to January 1, 1978.

What Is Copyright?

A copyright is actually a collection of five exclusive rights. These are: the right to reproduce the work, the right to prepare derivative works, the right of distribution, the right to perform the work, and the right to display it. The first right allows the owner to reproduce the work by any means. The scope of this right can be hard to define, especially when it involves photocopying, microfiche, videotape, and the like. Under the Copyright Act of 1976, others may reproduce protected works only if such reproduction involves either a fair or an exempted use as defined by the act, which I will be discussing later in this chapter.

Second is the right to prepare derivative works based on the copyrighted work. A derivative work is one that transforms or adopts the subject matter of one or more preexisting works. Thus, derivative works of a photograph might include use in a composite, as well as adaptations into another medium such as television, film, or a painting.

Third is the right to distribute copies to the public for sale or lease. However, once a photographer sells a print, the right to control the further use of that very print is, usually, ended. This should be distinguished from the copyright in the print which can only be conveyed in a signed writing. When you sell the print alone, you are selling the physical piece, not the right to reproduce it. This rule, known as the first-sale doctrine, does not apply if the work is merely in the possession of someone else temporarily such as by bailment, rental, lease, or loan. Bailment is the legal term for legal temporary possession of someone else's property; parking a car in a paid parking lot establishes a bailment; so does leaving a film with a developer. In these instances the copyright owner retains the right to control the further sale or other disposition of the work. Moreover, the first-sale doctrine does not apply if the copyright owner has a contract with the purchaser that restricts the purchaser's freedom to dispose of the work. In such a case, if the purchaser exceeds those restrictions, there may be liability. In this situation the copyright owner's remedy will be governed by contract law rather than copyright law.

You should distinguish between a sale of a print and a sale of the copyright in that print. If nothing is said about the copyright when the print is sold, you will retain the copyright. Since purchasers may not be aware of this, you may wish to call it to their attention either in the sales memorandum or on the back of the photo. If a license to reprint is granted, it should be in writing and you should be very specific about its scope. For example, may a person who has purchased the right to use a photograph in a newspaper ad also use it in a magazine? Generally, the answer is no, but you should be clear in defining the boundaries of permissible uses.

Fourth is the right to perform the work publicly—for example, in the case of an audio/visual work, to broadcast a film on television, or show it in a theater.

Fifth is the right to display the work publicly. Once the copyright owner has sold a copy of the photograph, however, the owner of the copy has the right to display that copy but generally does not have permission to reproduce or transmit it.

Who Owns the Copyright?

The general rule regarding ownership of copyright is that the *photographer*—the creator—of an image is the owner of the copyright in it. Under the old law, which still applies to photographs taken before January 1, 1978, when a photograph was sold, ownership of a common-law copyright was presumed to pass to the purchaser of that photograph unless the photographer explicitly provided otherwise in a written agreement. In other words, there was a presumption in the law that a sale included not only the photograph itself, but all rights in that work. However, by specifically granting a customer only the nonexclusive use rights of a copy of the photograph (for instance, to use a photograph in an advertisement), the photographer would have retained the copyright, since such permission is not equivalent to assignment of the copyright.

Before the Copyright Act of 1976, the employer, subject, boss, client, or customer owned the negative, all prints, and all use rights in a photograph unless the parties contractually agreed otherwise. Thus, the customer owned the negative and the right to sell or license the use of the negative, or the right to use it himself commercially or in advertising.

In *White Studio, Inc.* v. *Dreyfoos* (for a table of cases, see Appendix II), the court held that the agreement between a photographer and customer constitutes a contract pursuant to which photographers are employees of their customers. Under this view, both conception and production of the photograph were work done for the customer and thus the customer was the exclusive owner of all proprietary rights. Later, in 1946, a court ruled that custom and usage could not be set up to oppose or alter a general principle or rule of law in order to modify the general rule that all proprietary rights to photographs vest in the customer.

The case of *Colten* v. *Jacques Marchais, Inc.* specifically extended to photography the rule that all rights in a picture belonged to the customer. The court held that the relationship between a commercial photographer and an advertising agency was no different from that between a portrait photographer and a customer.

Although a photographer was allowed to retain possession of the negative, the photographer did not have the right to print additional copies from it. This policy was based on either the theory of an implied contractual restriction or on the grounds of right of privacy.

Since 1978, an independent photographer would own the copyright in the work he or she created, unless otherwise expressly agreed to the contrary. Notwithstanding this fact, the photographer may still not be able to reproduce the work for commercial purposes without the consent of the person photographed due to the privacy laws.

The Copyright Act of 1976 reverses the presumption that the sale of a photograph carries the copyright with it. Today, unless there is a written agreement that transfers the copyright to the customer, the photographer retains the copyright.

Joint Works

If a photographer owns the copyright, he or she also automatically owns the exclusive rights. The photographers of a joint work are co-owners of the copyright in the work. A joint work is a work prepared by more than one person "with the intention that their contributions be merged into inseparable or interdependent parts of a unitary whole." Thus, whatever profit one creator makes from use of the work must be shared equally with the others unless they have a written agreement that states otherwise. If there is no intention to create a unitary, or indivisible, work, each creator may own the copyright to that creator's individual contribution. For example, one creator may own the rights to written material and another the rights in the illustrative photographs.

Theatrical works, for example, are generally considered joint works under the act, co-authored by the script writer, composer, lyricist, set designer, choreographer, director, and others who contribute their talent to the final production. The owners of the copyrights in a theatrical work may vary according to the contracts between the producer and the individual authors who contribute to the work.

Works for Hire

Works considered to be *works for hire* are an important exception to the general rule that a photographer owns the copyright in a picture he or she has taken. If a photograph was taken by an employee on the job, the law considers the picture a work for hire, and the employer will own the copyright. However, the parties involved may avoid application of this rule if they write their contract carefully. If the employment contract itself provides, for example, that creating the copyrightable material in question is not part of the "scope of employment," the employee will likely be considered the owner of the copyright and the work for hire doctrine will not apply, i.e., if a fashion photographer working for a fashion magazine takes pictures of an accident scene on his own time. Another method of achieving this same result is for the employee to have the copyright in the work expressly assigned back to him or her.

In *Peregrine* v. *Lauren Corp.*, the court found that a photographer was working for hire when the employing advertising agency had the right to supervise and control the photographer's work. Courts also consider the amount of an employer's artistic advice before, during, and after the photographic session when determining whether a photographer is working for hire as opposed to working as an independent contractor. (An independent contractor is someone hired on a one-time or job-by-job basis, as opposed to a permanent employee.) However, a professional portrait photographer is not considered as creating works for hire and always owns the copyright in the photographs.

If the photographer is an independent contractor, the photographs will be considered works for hire only if (1) the parties have signed a written agreement to that effect; and (2) the work is specially ordered or commissioned as a contribution to a collective work, as part of a motion picture or other audiovisual work, as a supplementary work, as a compilation, as a translation, as an instructional text, as answer material for a test, or as an atlas. Thus, if there is no contractual agreement to the contrary, the photographer who is an independent contractor will own the copyright on these works.

In *CCNV* v. *Reid* (1989), the Court made it clear that determining the status of the person creating the work, as either an employee or independent contractor, must be made by considering the following factors: the hiring party's right to control the manner and means by which the product is accomplished; the skill required; the source of the instrumentalities and tools; the location of the work; the duration of the relationship between the parties; whether the hiring party has the right to assign additional projects to the hired party; the extent of the hired party's discretion over when and how long to work; the method of payment; the hired party's role in hiring and paying assistants; whether the work is part of the regular business of the hiring party; whether the hiring party is in business; the provision of employee benefits; and the tax treatment of the hired party.

The Court also pointed out that if the copyrightable work is created by an independent contractor and the parties do not comply with § 101 by having a written agreement on works within the nine categories enumerated in that section, then the independent contractor will retain the copyright in the work unless the parties agreed that the contributions of each shall be for the purpose of creating a unitary work. In this latter situation the parties will be considered joint authors. This means that each has a right to exploit or use the copyrighted material, although any profits must be shared with the joint author. In other words, joint authorship is a form of partnership which will result in a loss of control of the work to the joint author.

In 1991, in a case entitled *Marco* v. *Accent Publishing Co.*, the United States Court of Appeals for the Third Circuit held that a freelance photographer working for a client on a commission basis, could not be considered the client's employee, but rather was an independent contractor. As such, the photographer retained his copyright rights in his images.

The court, in agreeing with the American Society of Media Photographers (ASMP), who had filed an amicus brief, held that almost every aspect of the photographer's relationship with the client supported this conclusion: the photographer used his own equipment, paid his own overhead, kept his own hours, paid his own taxes, and was a skilled worker.

Similarly, in 1992, the United States Court of Appeals for the Second Circuit held that a computer programmer was not an employee of a retailer that contracted with him to create a series of computer programs; therefore, the programmer, an independent contractor, was the author and owner of the work he created.

Transferring or Licensing the Copyright

A copyright owner may sell the entire copyright or any part of it, or may license any right within it. To accomplish this there must be a written document that describes the rights conveyed. The document should be signed by the copyright owner or the owner's duly authorized agent. A license authorizing a particular use of a work can be granted orally, but it will be revocable at the will of the copyright owner. In addition to reducing a license to writing, the scope of rights granted should be clear. Is the purchaser of a license permitted only a one-time use or multiple uses? By specifying the exact uses conveyed, a battle over rights often can be avoided.

It is not uncommon for a photographer to become the assignee or licensee of another person's copyright. This could happen, say, when a photographer wishes to incorporate another person's illustrations, photographs, recordings, writings, or other work into his or her work; in this case the photographer will often enter into a licensing agreement or assignment of ownership with the other person. Such an agreement is necessary to authorize use of the copyrighted work.

Both an assignment of ownership and a licensing agreement can, and should, be recorded with the Copyright Office. When the transaction is recorded, the rights of the assignee or licensee are protected by recording a deed—in much the same way as the rights of an owner of real estate are protected. In a case of conflicting transfers of rights, if both transactions are recorded within one month of the execution, the person whose transaction was completed first will prevail. If the transactions are not recorded within a month, the one who records first will prevail. A nonexclusive license will prevail over any unrecorded transfer of ownership. Finally, before a transferee (either an assignee or licensee) can sue a third party for infringement, the document of transfer must be recorded. The cost to record a transfer is only twenty dollars and is tax-deductible if it is a business expense. Considering the potential consequences of not recording a transfer of rights, the assignee or licensee is well advised to record.

One section of the 1976 Copyright Act pertains to the involuntary transfer of a copyright. This section, which states that such a transfer will be held invalid, was included primarily because of problems arising from U.S. recognition of foreign copyrights. For example, if a country did not want a photographer's controversial work to be published, it could claim to be the copyright owner and thereby refuse to license foreign publications. Under the act, the foreign government must produce a signed record of the transfer before its ownership will be recognized. This section does not apply to a transfer by the courts in a bankruptcy proceeding or a foreclosure of a mortgage secured in the copyright.

Termination of Copyright Transfers and Licenses

It has not been unusual for a photographer confronted with an unequal bargaining position vis-a-vis an ad agency to transfer all rights in the copyright to the agency for a pittance, only to see the work become valuable at a later date. The 1976 Copyright Act, in response to this kind of apparent injustice, provides that after a certain period has lapsed, the photographer or certain other parties may terminate the transfer of the copyright and reclaim the rights. Thus, the new act grants the photographer a second chance to exploit a work after the original transfer of copyright. This right to terminate a transfer is called a *termination interest.*

In most cases, the termination interest will belong to the photographer. But if the photographer is no longer alive and is survived by a spouse but no children, the surviving spouse owns the termination interest. If the deceased photographer is not survived by a spouse, ownership of the interest belongs to any surviving children in equal shares. If the decedent is survived by both spouse and children, the interest is divided so that the spouse receives fifty percent and the children receive the remaining fifty percent in equal proportions.

Where the termination interest is owned by more than one party, be they other photographers or a photographer's survivors, a majority of the owners must agree to terminate the transfer. Under the new act, the general rule is that termination may be effected at any time within a five-year period beginning at the end of the thirty-fifth year from the date on which the rights were transferred. If, however, the transfer included the right of publication, termination may go into effect at any time within a five-year period beginning at the end of thirty-five years from the date of publication, or forty years from the date of transfer, whichever is shorter.

The party wishing to terminate the transferred interest must serve an advance written notice on the transferee. This notice must state the intended termination date and must be served not less than two and no more than ten years prior to the stated termination date. A copy of the notice must be recorded in the Copyright Office before the effective date of termination.

What Can Be Copyrighted?

The Constitution authorizes Congress to provide protection for a limited time to "authors" for their "writings." An author, from the point of view of copyright law, may be the creator—be it a photographer, sculptor, writer, or the employer in a work-for-hire situation; there have been debates over what constitutes a writing, but it is now clear that this term includes photographs. Congress avoided use of the word "writings" in describing the scope of copyright protection. Instead it grants copyright protection to "original works of authorship fixed in any tangible medium of expression." Legislative comments on this section of the act suggest that Congress chose to use this wording rather than writings in order to have more leeway to legislate in the copyright field.

Within these broad limits, the medium in which a work is executed does not affect its copyrightability. Section 102 contains a list of copyrightable subject matter, which includes: (1) literary works; (2) musical works, including any accompanying words; (3) dramatic works, including any accompanying music; (4) pantomimes and choreographic works; (5) pictorial, graphic, and sculptural works; (6) motion pictures and other audiovisual works; (7) sound recordings; and (8) architectural works. Yet this list is not intended to be exhaustive, and courts are free to recognize as protectable types of works not expressly included in the list.

The 1976 act expressly exempts from copyright protection "any idea, procedure, process, system, method of operation, concept, principle, or discovery." In short, a copyright extends only to the *expression* of creations of the mind, not to the ideas themselves. Frequently there is no clear line of division between an idea and its expression, a problem which will be considered in greater detail in the "Infringement and Remedies" section of this chapter. For now, it is sufficient to note that a pure idea, such as a plan to photograph something in a certain manner, cannot be copyrighted no matter how original or creative it is.

The law and the courts generally avoid using copyright law to arbitrate the public's taste. Thus, a work is not denied a copyright even if it makes no pretense to aesthetic or academic merit. The only requirements are that a work be original and show some creativity. Originality—as distinguished from uniqueness—requires that a photograph be taken independently, but does not require that it be the only one of its kind. In other words, a photograph of underwater algae in the Antarctic is copyrightable for its creative aspects; the unusual, hard-to-shoot subject matter is irrelevant.

In the past, the Copyright Office occasionally denied protection to works considered immoral or obscene, even though it had no express authority for doing so. Today this practice has changed. The Copyright Office will not attempt to decide whether a work is obscene or not, and copyright registration will not be refused because of the questionable character of any work.

Not everything in a copyrighted work is protected. Photographers should be aware that, for example, the title of a photograph cannot be copyrighted. Writers have the problem of whether a fictional character can be protected by copyright.

Under the 1909 act, most photographs that qualified for copyright had to be published with the proper notice attached in order to get statutory protection. The 1976 act dramatically changes the law in this respect. A photographer's pictures are now automatically copyrighted once they are "fixed in a tangible medium of expression." The photographer's product is considered to have been fixed in a tangible medium of expression as soon as he clicks the shutter and an image is created on film. The photograph need not be developed to be protected. However, after the 1976 act and prior to the 1988 amendment (effective March 1, 1989), a copyright could be lost if a photograph was published without the proper notice, unless the "savings clause" from Section 405 of the act applied. (The savings clause enables a photographer to save a copyright in certain situations.) For further discussion of retrieving copyright protection after publication without notice prior to March 1, 1989, see "Deposit and Registration" later in this chapter.

Once the copyright on a work has expired, or been lost, the work enters the public domain, where it can be exploited by anyone in any manner. A photographer can, however, get a copyright on a work derived from a work in the public domain if a distinguishable variation is created. This means, for example, that Rembrandt's *Night Watch* cannot be copyrighted, but a photograph of it can. As a result, no one would be able to copy the photograph, whereas anyone can copy Rembrandt's original. The photograph is thus a copyrightable derivative work of a preexisting work. Other examples of copyrightable derivative works would include collages, photographs of photographs, film versions, and any other work "recast, transformed, or adapted" from an original. If the copy was identical in all particulars so as to be indistinguishable from the original and the copying involved no creativity or originality, it would not be a derivative work and, therefore, not copyrightable.

Compilations are also copyrightable, as long as the preexisting materials are gathered and arranged in a new or original form. Compilations such as magazines, pamphlets, or books can be copyrightable as a whole even though individual contributions or photographs are individually copyrighted.

Publication

In copyright law, the concept of publication is different from what a lay person might expect it to be. Publication, according to the 1976 act, is the distribution of copies of a work to the public by sale or other transfer of ownership, or by rental, lease, or loan. Thus, a public performance or display of a work does not of itself constitute publication. And, under the doctrine of limited publication, which was part of the 1909 act, publication will not be deemed to have occurred when a photographer displays work "to a definitely selected group and for a limited purpose, without the right of diffusion, reproduction, distribution or sale."

Thus, when a photographer showed copies of a picture to close friends or associates with the understanding that such copies were not to be further reproduced and distributed, the photographer had not published the pictures, nor would the distribution of pictures to agents or customers for purposes of review and criticism constitute a publication. Even an exhibition in a gallery or museum where copying or photographing the work was prohibited probably would not have constituted publication. In *American Tobacco Co.* v. *Werckmeister*, the Supreme Court held that museum exhibition was not publication even though admission was charged because copying and photographing of the work was prohibited.

The revised act of 1976 makes no specific reference to this doctrine of limited publication. The statutory definition of publication does, however, require a "distribution of copies or phonorecords of a work to the public." Moreover, a congressional report on the revised act states that "the public" in this context refers to people who are under no explicit or implicit restrictions with respect to disclosure of the work's contents. This appears to suggest a continuation of the doctrine of limited publication under the current act. As will be seen later, publication is important since it identifies the point when proper use of the copyright notice (discussed later in this chapter) will defeat certain defenses which may be raised to excuse an unauthorized use of a copyrighted work.

Duration of Copyright

The duration of copyright depends upon when and how the work was created. In general, if the author is an individual, works created on or after the effective date of the 1976 act, January 1, 1978, will have copyright protection from the instant of creation until fifty years after the author's death. For works created jointly, the period is measured by the life of the last surviving author plus fifty years. The copyright in works made for hire and for anonymous or pseudonymous works lasts seventy-five years from the year of first publication, or one hundred years from the year of the work's creation, whichever period expires first. Unlike the 1909 act, the 1976 act requires no renewal. Renewal of copyrights in works first published prior to January 1, 1978, however, was required in the twenty-eighth year after first publication.

A law providing for the automatic renewal of such works was enacted in June 1992.

Creation of Copyright

As discussed earlier, all works are now automatically protected by the federal copyright law as soon as they are fixed in a tangible medium. There are no formal requirements of registration or deposit of copies in order to obtain copyright. Unpublished works can be registered with the Copyright Office, and it is necessary that registration have taken place if an infringement suit is going to be filed. The prepublication registration can be made after the infringement, though, as long as the registration occurs before filing suit. One of the advantages to early registration is that after five years the facts contained in the registration are presumed to be true in an infringement case. This presumption, which will carry over even after the work is published, can greatly simplify the copyright owner's preparation for trial.

Copyright Notice

Works published under the 1909 act had to contain the proper notice in order to be copyrighted. With few exceptions, any omission, misplacement, or imperfection in the notice on any copy of a work distributed by authority of the copyright owner placed the work forever in the public domain. Thus it was important for the copyright owner, when signing a contract, to make sure that granting a license to publish be conditioned on the publisher's inclusion of the proper copyright notice. That way, if the publisher made a mistake in the notice, the publication might be deemed unauthorized but the copyright would not be affected. The publisher could be liable to the copyright owner for the loss of copyright if it did occur.

Since notice is an inflexible requirement for works published before January 1, 1978, it is important to determine when publication occurred. Although notice is no longer required under the new law, the publication date is still of some importance. For example, the duration of the copyright of a work for hire is measured from either creation or first publication.

Location of Copyright Notice

The 1909 act contained complicated rules for the proper placement of the copyright notice within the work. Improper placement was one more error that was fatal to the copyright. Since March 1, 1989, a copyright notice is no longer required to be affixed to a work, nevertheless, it is a good idea to use the notice since it will make others aware of your rights and use of the notice will prevent one from claiming that the copyright was innocent or permissible under the doctrine of "innocent infringement" to be discussed later. The Copyright Office had required that the copyright notice for a photograph appear either on the front or back of the image or, in the case of a transparency, on the cardboard frame. A rubber stamp can make the job easy and it may be more legible.

Wording of a Copyright Notice

Even though it is no longer necessary to place a notice on your work, it still should be used whenever possible. A copyright notice has three elements. First there must be the word *copyright*, the abbreviation *Copr.*, or the letter *c* in a circle, ©. No variations are permitted. Second is the year of first publication (or, in the case of unpublished works governed by the 1909 act, the year in which the copyright was registered; the year of first publication should be used for unpublished works governed by the 1976 act). This date may be expressed in Arabic or Roman numerals or in words. Under the 1909 act it was not clear when a derivative (or revised) work—for example, a composite of photographs in a collage—was first published. To be safe, both dates, that of the original work and that of the revision, were usually given. The 1976 act makes it clear that the date of the first publication of the revised work is sufficient. The year of the first publication can be omitted on certain works designated in the act, but this category is extremely narrow. Since the year of first publication is necessary for some international protection, it should always be included. The third necessary element, following the date of publication, is the name of the copyright owner. If there are several, one name is sufficient. Usually the author's full name is used, but if the author is well known by a last name, the last name can be used alone or with initials. The same is true if the author is known by initials alone. A business that owns a copyright may use its trade name if the name is legally recognized in its state.

Copyright notice should be used to avoid having someone copy the work in the belief it is in the public domain. Even though the 1976 act allows the photographer to save the copyright on works published without notice and the 1989 revision does not require notice, someone who copies work believing it in the public domain because there is no notice is considered an innocent infringer under the statute. In this situation, the photographer whose work was copied cannot recover damages; in fact, a court might allow the copier to continue using the work. The 1989 amendment also provides that if the notice is used, then there is a presumption that an infringer cannot be innocent.

If international protection is desired, the copyright owner may have to add to the copyright notice. For example, under the Buenos Aires

Convention (which includes most Central and South American countries as well as the United States), the statement *all rights reserved*, in either Spanish or English, must be included in the notice. If there is any possibility that the work will be sold in Central or South America, it would be advisable to include this statement. Another agreement, the Universal Copyright Convention (UCC), requires the use of the international copyright symbol, ©, accompanied by the name of the copyright owner and the year of first publication. If these requirements are met, any formalities required by the domestic law of a UCC signatory country are deemed to have been satisfied. The protection in the country where the work is sold will then be the same as whatever protection that country accords its own nationals. Most European nations have signed the UCC, as has the United States. However, UCC protection is available only for American works first published in the United States after the convention became effective, which was on September 16, 1955. Thus, works first published in the United States before that date are not entitled to UCC protection. Nevertheless, such works will have international protection under another agreement—the Berne Convention—if the works were simultaneously published in the U.S. and a Berne signatory country.

In 1988, the United States became a party to the Berne Convention, which prohibits a signatory nation from requiring a copyright notice to be placed on a work as a condition for copyright protection. The U.S. Copyright Law was therefore amended effective March 1, 1989, to permit copyright protection without notice. It must be emphasized, however, that it is still prudent to use the notice for certain international protections (U.C.C.) and to prevent any innocent infringement.

Errors in or Omission of a Copyright Notice

Failure to give copyright notice or publishing an erroneous notice had very serious consequences under the old law. Under the 1909 act, the copyright was lost if the wrong name appeared in the notice. If the creator sold the copyright and recorded the sale, either the creator's or the new owner's name could be used. But if the sale was not recorded with the Copyright Office, use of the subsequent owner's name in the notice destroyed the copyright.

Under the 1976 act, a mistake in the name appearing in the notice is not fatal to the copyright. However, an infringer who was honestly misled by the incorrect name could use this as a defense to a suit for copyright infringement if the proper name was not on record with the Copyright Office. This is obviously another incentive for registering a sale or license of a copyright with the Copyright Office.

Under the 1909 act, a mistake in the year of the first publication also could have serious consequences. If an earlier date was used, the copyright term would be measured from that year, thereby decreasing the duration of protection. If a later date was used, the copyright was forfeited and the work entered the public domain. But because of the harsh consequences of losing a copyright, a mistake of one year was not penalized.

Under the 1976 act, using an earlier date will not be of any consequence when the duration of the copyright is determined by the author's life. When the duration of the copyright is determined by the date of first publication, as in the case of a composite work or work for hire, the earlier date will be used to measure how long the copyright will last. If a later year is used, the work is considered to have been published without notice.

Under the 1976 act, if a work was published between January 1, 1978 and March 1, 1989, without notice, the copyright owner is still protected for five years. If during those five years the owner registers the copyright with the Copyright Office and makes a reasonable effort to place a notice on copies of the photograph that were published without notice and distributed within the United States, full copyright protection will be granted for the appropriate duration of the published work. To place a notice on copies no longer in your possession, notify agencies, stores, or owners about the oversight and send out enough adhesive stickers for them to attach to all copies with the copyright information. If the notice has been omitted only from a relatively small number of copies, the owner need not register at all. However, risk of loss of copyright is not worth the gamble on how many copies constitute a "relatively small number." If there is any doubt, the photographer should register and attempt to get the omitted notice placed on copies that do not contain it.

A copyright owner is forgiven for an omission of notice if the omission was in violation of a contract that gave someone else the right to publish but required inclusion of the proper notice as a condition of publishing. (In other words, the copyright holder had fulfilled the responsibility for notice and is not held responsible for the other person's oversight.) Also, if the notice is removed or obliterated by an unauthorized person, this will have no effect on the validity of the copyright.

Since the purpose of the notice is to inform members of the public that the copyright owner possesses the exclusive rights granted by the statute, it is logical that someone who infringes these rights should not be penalized if the error was made because of the absence of the notice. Even though notice is not required after March 1, 1989, its use will deprive a copier of the ability to argue that an infringement was innocent. In some cases, the "innocent" infringer may be compelled to give up any profits made from the infringement. On the other hand, if the innocent infringer has made a sizable investment for future production, the court may compel the copyright owner to grant a license to the infringer.

Deposit and Registration

While a copyright notice on a photograph tells viewers who holds the copyright, it does not constitute official notice to the United States government. Once a photograph has been published, depositing the work and registering an application for copyright should be taken care of.

Depositing a work and registering an application are two different acts. Neither is a prerequisite for creating a federal copyright; as a general rule, copyright protection is automatic when an idea is "fixed in a tangible medium of expression," and, because of the copyright notice, copyright protection remains with the work after it is published or distributed to the public.

The obvious question, then, is why bother to deposit the work and file the application? As will be seen later, registration is required as a prerequisite to filing a lawsuit and may be necessary in order for you to obtain certain copyright remedies. In addition, there is a statutory presumption that the copyright is valid if the work has been registered.

Under the *deposit section* of the new law, the owner of the copyright or the owner of the exclusive right of publication (usually a publisher or advertiser) must deposit in the Copyright Office, for the use of the Library of Congress, two copies of the "best edition" of the work within three months after the work has been published. In the case of an unpublished work, or a collective work, only one copy need be deposited. The copies or copy should be sent to the Register of Copyrights, Library of Congress, Washington, D.C. 20559. This basic deposit requirement also applies to works published abroad when such works are either imported into the United States or become part of an American publication.

If the two copies are not deposited within the requisite three-month period, the Register of Copyrights may demand them. (The Register of Copyrights is not omniscient; the office would likely know that a particular photograph had been published because of other correspondence with a publisher. If you have published a photograph on your own and never corresponded with the office, it is not likely that this demand will be made.) If the copies are not submitted within three months after demand, the person upon whom demand was made may be subject to a fine of up to $250 for each unsubmitted work. In addition, such person or persons may be required to pay the Library of Congress an amount equal to the retail cost of the work, or, if no retail cost has been established, the costs incurred by the library in acquiring the work, provided such costs are reasonable. Finally, a copyright proprietor who willfully and repeatedly refuses to comply with a demand may be liable for an additional fine of $2,500.

Depositing copies under the deposit section of the new law is not a condition of copyright protection, but in light of the penalty provisions, it would indeed be foolish not to comply, if asked.

The *registration section* of the 1976 act requires that the copyright proprietor complete an application form, obtained from the Register of Copyrights at the Library of Congress, and pay a twenty-dollar registration fee. Photographers should use the form VA to register the copyright in a photograph. The form is brief and straightforward; the instructions accompanying it are short and easy to understand. In addition, the proprietor must deposit two copies of the "best edition" of the work to be registered (one copy if the photograph is unpublished).

The photographer must title each picture. If you have many pictures whose copyright you wish to register, you can save time and money by registering and copyrighting them as a single group and, rather than titling each photograph, titling the group. The title need not be impressive; it can be as simple as "1995 photographs." All works in the group must be created in the same year and if published must have been published together. It is also essential that the images be clear and the assemblage have a sufficiently orderly form and consistency of theme to bear a single title. Because internal rules of the Copyright Office are subject to change, a photographer is wise to check with the office as to what constitutes currently acceptable bulk registration practices. Bulk filings of published works may be subject to stricter requirements than bulk filings of unpublished works.

As an alternative to bulk filing in group form, the photographer could print many negatives on a single contact sheet and thus register the copyright in all of the photos on the single sheet for the cost of only one registration. Again, each photo need not be separately titled as long as the contact sheet includes an appropriate title.

Once a work has been registered as unpublished it does not need to be registered again when published. Often, a photograph's first public appearance is as part of a copyrighted collective work such as a book or magazine. If, as is usually the case, the author or publisher of the collective work and the photographer intend that the photographer will own the copyright in the photographs, the photographer can register the copyright directly on form VA. However, the photographer must file a copy of the entire collective work in which the photograph appears. Also, a large collection of one photographer's contributions to various collective works can be registered under a single application if all the work was published within a twelve-month period, and a copy of each photo as it appeared in each collective work is deposited with the application. If the work was created before March 1, 1989, it is also required that each piece have appeared in the collective works with a proper copyright notice in the photographer's name. In order to accomplish this type of bulk registration, the photographer must complete a form and then list each photograph separately on a GR/CP form.

There is an alternative method of protecting photographs that appear in separately copyrighted collective works. The publisher of the collective work and the photographer may choose to view the publisher as holding the copyright to the photographs, subject to a contractual obligation to assign the copyright to the photographer. This assignment should be executed in writing and filed with the Copyright Office. The advantage of using the assignment process to establish the photographer's copyright is that there is no need for the photographer to submit a copy of the collective work or a copy of the photograph to the Copyright Office. This method presupposes that the collective work was deposited and registered by the publisher before the photographer registered the assignment.

Although registration is not a condition to copyright protection, the 1976 act specifies that the copyright owner cannot bring a lawsuit to enforce his or her copyright until the copyright has been registered. Additionally, if the copyright is registered after an infringement occurs, the owner's legal remedies will be limited. If the copyright was registered prior to the infringement, the owner may be entitled to more complete remedies, including attorney's fees and statutory damages. No remedies will be lost if registration is made within three months of publication. Thus, the owner of a copyright has a strong incentive to register the copyright at the earliest possible time, certainly within the three-month grace period.

Proof of Registry and Copyright

You will know your registration and copyright have been accepted when the Copyright Office returns the form you submitted with a registration number on it. Probably there will be no accompanying information and it may look informal; nevertheless this will be an official document, to be stored in a safe place. The effective date of registration is when the form, fee, and deposit are received together at the Copyright Office.

Copyright Infringement and Remedies

A copyright infringement occurs any time an unauthorized person exercises any of the exclusive rights protected by a copyright. The fact that the infringing party did not intend to improperly use protected rights or did not know that the work was protected by copyright is relevant only with respect to the penalty. All actions for infringement of copyright must be brought in a federal court within three years of the date of the infringement. The copyright owner must prove that the work is copyrighted and registered, that the infringer had access to and used the copyrighted work, and that the infringer copied a "substantial and material" portion of the copyrighted work. In order to demonstrate the extent of the damage caused by the infringement, the copyright owner must also provide evidence that shows how widely the infringing copies were distributed.

The copyright owner must prove that the infringer had access to the protected work, because an independent creation of an identical work is not an infringement. However, infringement can occur even if an entire work was not copied because any unauthorized copying of a substantial portion of a work constitutes an infringement.

Obviously, direct reproduction of a photograph without the copyright holder's permission constitutes infringement. Less obviously, a drawing or painting based entirely on a copyrighted photograph can constitute an infringement if it is substantially similar. Also, a photographer who purposely and intentionally imitates and copies the copyrighted photograph of another is guilty of infringing the copyright. Photographers should be aware that in certain circumstances they may be liable for infringing copyrights of pictures they shot themselves. In *Gross* v. *Seligman*, the court held that a photographer infringed the copyright owned by a publisher of a photograph the same photographer had taken earlier; when the photographer reshot the same model in a similar pose, infringement occurred. (The court noted that the later picture differed from the earlier only in that the model was older and had more wrinkles.)

If the expression of ideas, rather than simply the ideas alone, is found to be similar, the court must decide whether the similarity is substantial. This is done in two steps. First, the court looks at the more general similarities of the works, such as subject matter, setting, materials used, and the like. Expert testimony may be offered here. The second step involves a subjective judgment of the works' intrinsic similarity: Would a lay observer recognize that the alleged copy had been appropriated from the copyrighted work? No expert testimony is allowed in making this determination.

A case in the late eighties, *Horgan* v. *Macmillan, Inc.*, holds that the substantial similarity test applies even when the allegedly infringing material is in a different medium. George Balanchine choreographed *The Nutcracker* ballet and his estate receives royalties every time the ballet is performed. Macmillan prepared for publication a book of photographs which included sixty color pictures of scenes from a performance of *The Nutcracker*. In determining whether this constituted infringement, the court of appeals noted that the correct test is whether "the ordinary observer, unless he set out to detect the disparities, would be disposed to overlook them, and regard their aesthetic appeal as the same." Furthermore, the court noted, "Even a small amount of the original, if it is qualitatively significant, may be sufficient to be an infringement, although the full original could not be recreated from the excerpt."

Even before the trial, the copyright owner may be able to obtain a preliminary court order against an infringer. The copyright owner can petition the court to seize all copies of the alleged infringing work and the negatives that produced them. To do this, the copyright owner must file a sworn statement that the work is an infringement and provide a substantial bond approved by the court. After the seizure, the alleged infringer has a chance to object to the amount or form of the bond.

After the trial, if the work is held to be an infringement, the court can order the destruction of all copies and negatives, and enjoin future infringement. In addition, the copyright owner may be awarded damages. The copyright owner may request that the court award actual damages or statutory damages—a choice that can be made any time before the final judgment is recorded.

Actual Damages

Actual damages are the amount of the financial injury sustained by the copyright owner or, as in most cases, the profits made by the infringer. In proving the infringer's profits, the copyright owner need only establish the gross revenues received for the illegal exploitation of the work. The infringer then must prove any deductible expenses.

Statutory Damages

The amount of statutory damages is decided by the court, within specified limits: no less than $500 and no more than $20,000. The maximum possible recovery is increased to $100,000 if the copyright owner proves that the infringer knew that an illegal act was being committed. The minimum possible recovery is reduced to $200 if the infringer proves ignorance of the fact that the work was copyrighted. The court has the option to award the prevailing party its costs and attorneys' fees. As previously noted, statutory damages and attorneys' fees may not be awarded in cases where the copyright was not registered prior to infringement. Registration within three months of publication is treated as having occurred on the date of publication.

Criminal Enforcement

The U.S. Justice Department can prosecute a copyright infringer. If the prosecutor proves beyond a reasonable doubt that the infringement was committed willfully and for commercial gain, the infringer can be fined up to $100,000 and sentenced to jail for up to one year. There is also a fine of up to $2,500 for fraudulently placing a false copyright notice on a work, for removing or obliterating a copyright notice, or for knowingly making a false statement in an application for a copyright.

Fair Use

Not every copying of a protected work will constitute an infringement. There are two basic types of non-infringing use: fair use and exempted use.

The Copyright Act of 1976 recognizes that copies of a protected work "for purposes such as criticism, comment, news reporting, teaching (including multiple copies for classroom use), scholarship or research" can be considered fair use and therefore not an infringement. However, this list is not intended to be complete nor is it intended as a definition of fair use. Fair use, in fact, is not defined by the act. Instead, the act cites four factors to be considered in determining whether a particular use is or is not fair:

1. The purpose and character of the use, including whether it is for commercial use or for nonprofit educational purposes,
2. The nature of the copyrighted work,
3. The amount and substantiality of the portion used in relation to the copyrighted work as a whole,
4. The effect of the use upon the potential market for, or value of, the copyrighted work.

The act does not rank these four factors, nor does it exclude other factors in determining the question of fair use. In effect, all that the act does is leave the doctrine of fair use to be developed by the courts.

A classic example of fair use would be reproduction of one photograph from a photography book in a newspaper or magazine review of that book. Another would be the photographing of a copyrighted photograph as background.

In *Rogers* v. *Koons*, the Court of Appeals for the Second Circuit rejected a sculptor's argument that his use of a photograph as a model to make a sculpture, was fair use. Before sending the photograph to a workshop for the purpose of having a maquette created, the sculptor removed the plaintiff's copyright notice. The sculptor subsequently sold three wooden copies of the maquette for a total of $367,000. The court held that the copying was not fair use.

The 1968 case of *Time Inc.* v. *Bernard Geis Associates* involved Abraham Zapruder of Dallas, Texas who took home movies of President Kennedy's arrival in Dallas. Zapruder started the film as the motorcade approached; when the assassination occurred, he caught it all.

Zapruder had three copies made of this film; two he gave to the Secret Service solely for government use; one he sold to *Life* magazine. *Life* registered a copyright to the films and refused to allow publisher Bernard Geis Associates the right to use pictures from the film in a book. When the publisher reproduced frames in the film by charcoal sketches, *Life* sued for copyright infringement. The court found, however, that the publisher's use of the pictures was a fair use and outside the limits of copyright protection, reasoning that the public had an interest in having the fullest possible information available on the murder of President Kennedy. The court also noted that the book would have had intrinsic merit and salability without the pictures and that the publisher had offered to pay *Life* for its permission to use the pictures. The court also noted that *Life* sustained no injury because the publisher was not in competition with it.

Parody

Another area in which the fair use defense has been used successfully is in cases involving parody or burlesque. The courts have generally been sympathetic to the parodying of copyrighted works, often permitting incorporation of a substantial portion of a protected work. The test has traditionally been whether the amount copied exceeded that which was necessary to recall or "conjure up" in the mind of the viewers the work being parodied or burlesqued. In these cases the substantiality of the copy, and particularly the conjuring up test, may be more important than the factor of economic harm to the copyright proprietor. *Walt Disney Productions* v. *Air Pirates* involved publication of two magazines of cartoons entitled "Air Pirates Funnies" in which characters resembling Mickey and Minnie Mouse, Donald Duck, the Big Bad Wolf, and the Three Little Pigs were depicted as active members of a free-thinking, promiscuous, drug-ingesting counterculture. The court held that a parodist's First Amendment rights and desire to make the best parody must be balanced against the rights of the copyright owner and the protection of the owner's original expression. The judges explained that the balance is struck by giving the parodist the right to make a "copy" that is just accurate enough to conjure up the original. Since the Disney cartoon characters had widespread public recognition, a fairly inexact copy would have been sufficient to call them to mind to members of the viewing public. The court held that by copying the cartoon characters in their entirety, the defendants took more than what was necessary to place firmly in the reader's mind the parodied work and those specific attributes that were to be satirized.

In the *Campbell* v. *Acuff-Rose* case, however, the United States Supreme Court permitted a broader application of the parody defense. It allowed the musical group, 2 Live Cru, to convert the popular song "Pretty Woman" into one which was overtly sexual, without incurring any liability for infringement.

Photocopying

One area in which the limits of fair use are hotly debated is the area of photocopying. The Copyright Act provides, remember, that "reproduction in copies ... for purposes such as criticism, comment, news reporting, teaching (including multiple copies for classroom use), scholarship or research" *can* be a fair use, which leaves many questions. Reproduction of what? A piece of an image? Over half an image? An image no longer generally available? How many copies? To help answer these questions, several interested organizations drafted a set of guidelines for classroom copying in nonprofit educational institutions. These guidelines are not a part of the Copyright Act but are printed in the act's legislative history. Even though the writers of the guidelines defined the guide as "minimum standards of educational fair use," major educational groups have publicly expressed the fear that publishers would attempt to establish the guidelines as maximum standards beyond which there could be no fair use.

As all this demonstrates, it is not easy to define what sorts of uses are fair uses. Questions continue to be resolved on a case-by-case basis. Thus, a photographer should consult a lawyer where it appears that one of his or her works has been infringed or where the photographer intends to use someone else's copyrighted work. The lawyer can research what the courts have held in cases with similar facts.

Fair Use in the Video Industry

The first U.S. Supreme Court case to address the fair use doctrine under the Copyright Revision Act of 1976 was *Sony Corporation of America* v. *Universal City Studios, Inc., et al.*, in 1984. This case deals with the effect of home video recorders on copyrighted movies aired on TV, and it is an important step in defining the bounds of the fair use doctrine under the new law. Universal Studios sued Sony because Sony manufactures and sells home videotape recorders which are used to record copyrighted works shown on television. In a five-to-four decision, the Court stated that home video recording for noncommercial purposes is a fair use of copyrighted television programs.

The Supreme Court's analysis of fair use emphasized the economic consequences of home video recording to copyright owners. The Court looked to the first of the four factors listed in the 1976 Copyright Act as relevant to the fair use defense: "The purpose and character of the use." Consideration of this factor, reasoned the Court, requires a weighing of the commercial or nonprofit character of the activity. If the recorders had been used to make copies for commercial or profit-making purposes, the use would be unfair. But since video recording of television programs for private home use is a noncommercial, nonprofit activity, the court found that the use was a fair use.

The Court then considered "the effect of the use upon the potential market for or value of the copyrighted work," the fourth factor listed in the act. Here, the Court found that although copying for noncommercial reasons may impair the copyright holder's ability to get the rewards Congress intended, to forbid a use that has no demonstrable effect upon the potential market, or upon the value of the work, would merely prohibit access to ideas without any benefit.

The rule emerging here is that a challenge to noncommercial use of a copyrighted work requires proof that the use (1) is harmful to the copyright owner; or (2) would adversely affect the potential market for the copyrighted work should the use become widespread. In *Sony*, the Court concluded that Universal Studios had failed to prove actual or probable harm, and thus the recordings constituted fair use.

In this case, the alleged copyright infringement was the unauthorized recording or copying of the movies by home viewers. Several other recent video cases involve a slightly different situation: members of the public viewing video movies in what is alleged to be an unauthorized public performance. At least one lower court has held that copyright is not infringed when guests at a resort are allowed to rent video discs and view them in their rooms. However, two other courts have held that copyright *is* infringed when owners of video rental stores provide viewing rooms where members of the public can view the movies they have rented. The primary issue in all of these cases was whether the uses constituted public performances, not whether the uses were fair. Nevertheless, like the *Sony* case, they illustrate the difficult copyright issue presented by the video industry. Clearly this area of the law is still developing, and any photographer connected with the video market should consult with a lawyer to learn the extent of the photographer's control over his or her work.

Exempted Uses

In many instances the ambiguities of the fair use doctrine have been resolved by statutory exemptions. Exempted uses are those specifically permitted by statute in situations where the public interest in making a copy outweighs any harm to the copyright proprietor.

Libraries and Archives

Perhaps the most significant of these exemptions is the library and archives exemption, which basically provides that libraries and archives may reproduce and distribute a single copy of a work provided that (1) such reproduction and distribution is not for the purpose of direct or indirect commercial gain; (2) the collections of the library or archives are available to the public or available to researchers affiliated with the library or archives as well as to others doing research in a specialized field; and (3) the reproduction and distribution of the work includes a copyright notice.

According to the legislative history of the Copyright Act, Congress particularly encourages copying of films made before 1942 because these films are printed on film stock with a nitrate base that will decompose in time. Thus, so long as an organization is attempting to preserve our cultural heritage, copying of old films is allowed and encouraged under the fair use doctrine.

The exemption for libraries and archives is intended to cover only single copies of a work. It does not generally cover multiple reproductions of the same material, whether made on one occasion or over a period of time, and whether intended for use by one person or for separate use by the individual members of a group. Under interlibrary arrangements, various libraries may provide one another with works missing from their respective collections, unless these distribution arrangements substitute for a subscription or purchase of a given work.

This exemption in no way affects the applicability of fair use, nor does it apply where such copying is prohibited in contractual arrangements agreed to by the library or archives when it obtained the work.

Sovereign Immunity

A number of comparatively recent cases have involved the question of whether or not the federal government or any state can be liable for copyright infringement. Thus far, because of the doctrine of *sovereign immunity*, federal and state governments have been found to be protected against liability for infringement when using copyrighted work. Since the United States government or a state government can only be sued when it consents to be sued, the plaintiff must establish that the government authorized or consented to the infringement and that the government agreed to be sued for it.

Although the Copyright Remedy Clarification Amendment of 1990 provides that states can be held liable for copyright infringement, many cases have held that this amendment is prohibited by the Eleventh Amendment to the U.S. Constitution. Thus, a photographer may have work infringed by the state or federal government and have no redress. The immunity, however, may not extend to the individual responsible for the infringement. The United States Court of Appeals for the Fourth

Circuit has held that the Eleventh Amendment may shield a state university from liability for copyright infringement, but the publication director who used the infringing photo in the student catalogue may herself be liable.

Moral Rights

Photographic work as an art is a form of property requiring unique consideration. As a photographer, you have an interest in deciding whether to disclose your work, seeing that your work retains the form you gave it and ensuring that you are properly credited. While these rights indirectly affect the photographer's economic interests, they more basically affect the photographer's character and therefore generally are referred to as moral rights, or *droit moral*.

The artist's moral rights are recognized in eighty-one countries throughout the world, including the United States, and have been codified in the 1928 Berne Convention, discussed above. This Convention covers international copyright protection in addition to many other elements of the *droit moral*.

While moral rights principles are often considered antagonistic to the property rights of owners in the U.S., protection of certain minimal moral rights became mandatory when the United States became a signatory to Berne in 1988. Prior to that time, the U.S. had been a signatory to the Universal Copyright Convention, promulgated by the U.S. as a compromise to joining Berne in 1952.

In 1990, Congress passed the Visual Artists Rights Act (VARA), which amends the Copyright Act by providing to "authors" of certain works the rights of attribution and integrity. The act expressly includes photographs which are produced for exhibition purposes only as a signed single copy or signed, numbered, limited edition of two hundred or fewer. These rights may be enforced by any applicable remedy, other than criminal penalties, otherwise available for infringement under the Copyright Act. These rights belong solely to the photographer and are not transferable.

The Computer Age and Copyright

With the advent of new technology, there is a new arena emerging in which many of the legal issues presented throughout this text are being reexamined. The rights of publicity, libel, copyright, and privacy, as well as ethical considerations, are among the most prominent, although others keep surfacing.

A major concern for the photography profession is computer-enhanced imagery. Digital technology now enables a computer to produce vivid images which can be manipulated and distorted to varying degrees. As a result of the new innovations, many opportunities and risks are surfacing which have not been clearly delineated. While to date, there is no case law or statute directly on point, commentators and legal scholars have been active. There is a growing body of literature discussing the new technological advances and the many problems which are likely to confront the professional photographer.

If a photographic image is electronically captured and manipulated, at what point is it still substantially similar to the original form so as to give rise to liability for copyright infringement? While defining the boundaries of permissible copying is by no means a new problem, the new technology facilitates manipulation and, as a result, provides a broader array of possible conflicts.

Certainly, an identical copy, albeit in a different medium, would be an infringement. If the image is changed substantially, however, is it still considered an embodiment of the original idea?

There are also privacy issues which emerge. If, for example, a digitally scanned photo of an identifiable person is so distorted as to make that person unrecognizable—can the subject of the original photograph succeed in an invasion of privacy claim when the digital picture is commercially reproduced?

Similarly, does it infringe upon a celebrity's right of publicity to have their images digitally manipulated in this manner? In the early 1990s, television commercials featured contemporary entertainers such as Paula Abdul and Elton John singing and dancing with computerized images of deceased entertainers, including Louis Armstrong, Humphrey Bogart, and James Cagney. In many states, an entertainer's right of publicity ends when that person dies. Thus, the estates of the deceased stars would have no recourse in many jurisdictions even though it is highly unlikely that the 1990s advertisers obtained the deceased performers' consent to include them in the commercials. This also raises ethical issues for photographers who provide photographs which could be used to affect a deceased entertainer's reputation.

Concerns over the myriad of legal and ethical issues which may impact on the photography profession, prompted the American Society of Media Photographers (ASMP) to create a copyright licensing organization known as Media Photographers Copyright Agency (MP©A). The agency's goals are to raise standards and ensure fair practice in the field of photography. It is charged with responsibility for policing the use of its members' work.

For more information on MP©A, contact ASMP (see Appendix III for the address).

2

DEFAMATION
AND LIBEL

In the year 400 B.C., the Greek philosopher Socrates was convicted of teaching atheism to the children of Athens and was sentenced to death. Of the four hundred jurors, all but two voted for conviction. In his defense, Socrates claimed that most of the charges were based on lies and that his reputation had been unjustly attacked for years. For example, he argued, in *The Clouds*, a play by Aristophanes that was performed before the entire population of Athens, the bumbling teacher of philosophy was named Socrates. However, in Athens, free speech, other than heresy, was an absolute right, and Socrates had no protection against statements which today would be considered defamatory.

Despite the First Amendment guarantee that freedom of speech will not be abridged, in contemporary America that freedom is limited. Defamatory material which includes photographs is not absolutely protected—and is in fact prohibited by law in all fifty states. A statement will generally be considered defamatory if it tends to subject a person to hatred, contempt, or ridicule or if it results in injury to that person's reputation while in office, in business, or at work.

The American Law Institute defines libel as publication of defamatory matter "by written or printed words, by its embodiment in physical form (such as in photographs), or by any other form of communication which has the potentially harmful qualities characteristic of written or printed words." Photographs can, therefore, be defamatory. Generally, a picture by itself cannot be the basis for liability because truth is a defense to libel and the camera merely records what is there. However, photographs can become defamatory if they are airbrushed or otherwise altered in a way that exposes the subject to ridicule or contempt.

Photographs usually are published with accompanying text or captions. In determining whether or not a photograph is defamatory, the court will consider a publication in its entirety. To protect against liability for defamation, a photographer should caption photographs accurately before selling them. Also, the photographer should be careful not to participate in or explicitly approve of false or injurious text accompanying the photographs. In *Cantrell* v. *Forest City Publishing Co.*, a reporter wrote a story on the poverty of a family whose father had been killed in a flood. A photographer took fifty pictures of the family's home, some of which were published with the story. When the family sued, the photographer was not held liable because there was no evidence that he was involved in writing the defamatory text.

If defamation is written or tangible, it is *libel*; if it is oral, it is *slander*. For the most part the same laws and principles govern all defamatory statements, but since a photographer's liability involves images that appear on paper, we will focus here on libel. As a photographer, you must be cautious about any photographs or captions that might be considered defamatory. If the work is published—and as you will see, "published" has a very broad meaning in the context of libel—you, as the photographer, could be sued along with the publisher, under the libel statutes.

It is not always easy to determine whether a photograph is defamatory. In order to give you some idea of the scope of libel, let us take a closer look at what kinds of photographs the courts have found to be libelous. Then we will look at who can sue a photographer for libel, and various defenses a photographer can use against different plaintiffs.

Actionable Libel

Actionable libel is libel that would furnish legal grounds for a lawsuit. In order for a photograph to be libelous, it must, in legal terminology, *convey a defamatory meaning* about an identifiable person or persons, and must have been published. Thus, a photograph of, for example, a Jewish leader in which a Nazi armband has been air-brushed in would be libelous.

Courts have traditionally put libel into two categories: *libel per se* and *libel per quod*. In libel per se, the defamatory meaning is apparent from the statement or thing itself. In libel per quod, the defamatory meaning is conveyed only in conjunction with other material. In libel per quod, the photograph may be susceptible to more than one reasonable interpretation, but as long as any one of the interpretations is defamatory, the picture will be libelous.

Libel Per Se

One example of libel per se is an accusation of criminal or morally reprehensible acts. An accusation of criminal conduct is libelous per se even though it is not explicitly stated; if the photographer has published a photograph and captions that describe a crime or has cast suspicion by innuendo, that is sufficient for libel per se. In *Time, Inc.* v. *Ragano*, the court found potential defamation liability based on publication of a photograph of seven men seated at a restaurant table accompanied by an article that referred to the men, two of whom were attorneys, as Cosa Nostra hoodlums. Similarly, in *Hagler* v *Democrat News, Inc.*, a newspaper ran a photograph of a couple's beach cabin to illustrate an article on a drug raid. Because the photograph included a sign identifying the owners of the cabin, the owners sued for invasion of privacy and for defamation. As the pictured cabin was in no way implicated in the drug raid, the photograph would indeed have been defamatory had the text of the article not made it clear that the drug raid occurred in another cabin.

On the other hand, it is never libel per se to say that someone is exercising a legal right—even though the person may not want the fact known. For example, it is not libel per se to say or to imply by a photograph that a man killed someone in self-defense, that he brought a divorce suit against his wife, or that he invoked the Fifth Amendment forty times. Although these statements may cast suspicion, they cannot be libelous per se because they merely report the exercise of a legal right.

To state that someone has a loathsome or contagious disease such as syphilis, gonorrhea, or AIDS is libelous per se. A statement that describes deviant sexual conduct or unchastity, particularly by a woman, is libelous per se. In one case, the court found that publication of a woman's nude photograph, without her consent, in a magazine that promoted the careers of aspiring porn stars was defamatory. The suggestion of unwed pregnancy also undermines a woman's reputation for chastity and can be the basis for defamation action. In *Triangle Publications, Inc.* v. *Chumley*, a newspaper and magazine published a photograph of a teen-age girl embracing a man and a photograph of her alleged diary with an entry stating she was pregnant. These photos were part of an advertisement for a television series on teen pregnancy. The court held that the photographs were defamatory.

When the statement involves politics, the determination of libel per se is more difficult. Today, courts generally agree that a statement that a person belongs to a particular political group will be libel per se only if that group advocates the use of violence as a means of achieving political ends. Thus, to say that someone belongs to the Ku Klux Klan would probably be libel per se. But to say that someone is a racist would probably not be, since racism is not necessarily intertwined with the use of violence. In some instances, though, a photograph that makes a statement concerning someone's political affiliation may constitute libel per se regardless of the political group's attitude toward violence. For example, to depict someone as a communist may be libel per se because communist affiliation is generally injurious to a person's reputation within significant portions of society today.

It is usually deemed libel per se to impute to a professional person a breach of professional ethics, general unfitness or inefficiency. For example, it may be libel per se to indicate that a person's business is bankrupt, because the statement implies a general unfitness to do business. However, to indicate that the business person did not pay a certain debt is not libel per se, because everyone has a legal right to contest a debt. Similarly, it may be libel per se to imply that a doctor is a butcher, because it implies general incompetence. But it is not libel per se to imply that the doctor made a mistake, so long as it does not imply general incompetence. Everyone makes mistakes.

There is a gray area concerning statements or pictures about certain business practices that may not be illegal but which nonetheless could give a business bad publicity. To indicate someone is cutting prices would not be libel per se, but to indicate someone is cutting prices to drive a competitor out of business would be.

It is impossible to describe every situation that could constitute libel per se, since any situation can be libel per se if it is likely to produce a reprehensible opinion of someone in the minds of a large number of reasonable people. Remember, the rule of thumb is that a photograph or statement is libelous per se when the defamatory meaning is clear from the situation itself. Thus, a photograph of a person shaking hands with someone wearing a Ku Klux Klan costume and setting fire to a cross would be libel per se when the photographer skillfully imposed the image of a person who would not be involved with the Klan on to the photograph.

Libel: per Quod

In libel *per quod*, since the defamatory meaning is conveyed only in conjunction with other factors, the plaintiff who sues for libel must introduce the context of the situation and demonstrate to the court how the picture and caption, text, or other pictures as a whole result in a defamatory innuendo. For example, *Gomes* v. *Fried* involved a photograph that showed an officer sitting in his police car with his head tilted to one side, and it was accompanied by a caption reading: "Officer Gomes' car shown in the center of the lightly traveled Bristol Avenue (Sunday afternoon) prowling for traffic violations. His head tilted may suggest something." While the officer admitted that the photograph was accurate, the court observed that the innuendo in the caption made it potentially defamatory, suggesting to ordinary readers that the officer was sleeping on duty. In fact, as many readers stated in later letters to the newspaper, and as the officer himself testified, he was called "Sleepy" and known as the Sleeping Officer. Nevertheless, the codefendants, the editor and publisher of the newspaper, knew that the officer was not sleeping, but was writing a traffic citation at the time the photograph was taken. Thus, although the photograph was accurate, the court held that the photograph could be the basis for a suit.

Another example of a case involving libel per quod, was characterized as "libel by thank-you." In April 1993, a Los Angeles federal judge dismissed an unusual libel suit involving a high-powered Beverly Hills entertainment lawyer, Mickey Rudin, and celebrity author Kitty Kelley. Rudin charged Kelley with defaming him in her 1991 unauthorized biography of Nancy Reagan when Kelley thanked Rudin as one of the people she said had made "the most important contribution to this book." Specifically, Rudin argued that Kelley had maliciously listed him as a source to create the false impression that he revealed confidential information to Kelley about a relationship between Nancy Reagan and Frank Sinatra, a former client of Rudin's. Rudin is neither mentioned nor quoted in the book; his name appears only in the list of 612 sources and in footnotes to one chapter that refer to correspondence with Rudin. He maintained that he never spoke to Kelley nor provided any kind of assistance.

The judge dismissed Rudin's case, holding that Rudin failed to prove he had been damaged in the manner necessary under California law to sustain his claims of libel or invasion of privacy. The judge also rejected

Rudin's argument that Kelley violated the federal Lanham Act by falsely identifying him as a source, thereby giving the impression Rudin was associated with the book.

Defamatory Advertising and Trade Libel

Photographers should be aware that they are potentially liable for a type of defamation known as *trade libel* if they help to create advertisements that impugn the quality of commercial merchandise or products. If an advertisement reflects adversely on a competitor's character, it can constitute defamation per se. If the advertisement on its face implies that a competitor is fraudulent or dishonest, and if the competitor can prove financial loss, he or she may have an action for defamation per quod.

Proof of Damage

The distinction between libel per se and libel per quod is important primarily because it determines whether the plaintiff has to prove damage. Where there is libel per se, damage to reputation will be presumed and the plaintiff need not prove it. If, however, the charge is libel per quod, damage normally must be proved, although there are some exceptions to this general rule. If the innuendo in the libel per quod falls within one of four categories, damage will be presumed as in libel per se. The four categories are innuendos that (1) adversely reflect upon someone's ability to conduct a business, trade, or profession; (2) impute unchastity to an unmarried woman; (3) accuse someone of committing a crime of moral turpitude (a crime of moral turpitude is something that is immoral in itself, irrespective of the fact that it is punished by law; examples are rape and murder); or (4) accuse someone of having a loathsome disease such as leprosy or a venereal disease.

Publication

As mentioned earlier, a photograph must be published in order to constitute actionable libel. The legal meaning of *publication* in the libel context is very broad. Once a photograph is communicated to a third person who sees and understands it, the photograph, in the eyes of the law, has been published. Thus, if you show a photograph to someone other than the subject, you have published the photograph.

Generally, the person who is defamed can bring a separate lawsuit for each repetition of the defamatory photograph. However, when the photograph is contained in a book, magazine, or newspaper, a majority of courts have adopted what is known as the *single-publication rule*. Under this rule, a person cannot make each copy of the book grounds for a separate suit. Rather, the number of copies is taken into account only for purposes of determining the extent of damages.

Who Can Sue for Libel?

In order for someone to sue for libel, the photograph at issue must clearly depict or identify that person or entity. This is easy to prove, of course, when the plaintiff is identified by name in the text, caption, or legend where the plaintiff is clearly visible and identifiable in the photograph. But if a plaintiff is not identified by name, the plaintiff can prove that he or she was nonetheless "identified" by showing that a third party could reasonably infer that the photograph was of the plaintiff. For example, if the plaintiff had a very unique and distinctive tattoo and it was visible in the photograph, even though the plaintiff's face was not, then if the photograph was defamatory, the plaintiff would likely be able to establish that he or she was depicted in it.

The courts have uniformly held that groups, corporations, and partnerships can sue for libel just as an individual can. Although there has been disagreement among the states as to whether not-for-profit corporations should be protected, the trend seems to be to allow nonprofit corporations to sue when they are injured in their ability to collect or distribute funds.

If a defamatory picture is published depicting an identified group of people, the possibility of each member of that group having a good cause of action will depend on the size of the group and whether the photograph defames all or only a part of the group.

Where the group is composed of more than one hundred members, the individuals generally do not have a good cause of action. If, for example, someone published a photograph of thousands of people in a ball park audience and added a caption indicating that all depicted were thieves, it is unlikely that one person's reputation could be damaged as a result of the photograph. On the other hand, if that same caption described a small group of individuals in the photograph, those individuals could probably win a defamation suit, since they would be more likely to be subject to contempt, hatred, or ridicule as a result of the defamatory picture.

The individual members of a group might not prevail if the allegedly defamatory statement referred only to a portion of the group. If, for example, someone states that "some members" of a particular trade group shown in a photograph "are communists," the individual members probably cannot prevail in a defamation suit, since the statement is not all-inclusive, and since those included are not named. Again, the size of the group could affect the court's ruling. If the partially defamed group is small and the people are recognizable, it would be more likely that the reputation of each member had been damaged, even though the statement was not all-inclusive.

A photographer confronted with the question of whether or not to publish a work that identifies a person, group, or entity should make a two-step analysis. First, does the picture—with any caption or related material—defame a reputation? If the answer is no, then it may be safely published (assuming no other wrongful act such as copyright infringement or invasion of privacy is involved). If the answer is yes, the second step is to determine whether there is a valid defense.

Defenses to Libel

Since photographers often write captions or descriptions to accompany their photographs, you as a photographer need to know the situations in which you can defend your right to publish certain kinds of pictures. Even if a plaintiff proves defamation, publication, and damages (where damages must be proved), the photographer may nevertheless prevail in a lawsuit if he or she is able to establish a valid defense.

Truth
Truth is an absolute defense to a charge of defamation, although it may not protect against other charges such as invasion of privacy. It is not necessary for a potentially defamatory statement to be correct in every respect in order to be considered true. As long as the statement is true in all essential particulars, the defense will be acceptable. For example, if the caption "X robbed Bank A" appeared under a photograph of a bank robbery, it would be considered true, and therefore not actionable, even though the photograph was in fact of a robbery of Bank B. The essential fact is that X was guilty of robbing a bank, so it is irrelevant which bank was robbed.

Opinion
A second possible defense is that the supposedly defamatory material was one of *opinion* rather than fact. The rationale for this defense is that one's opinion can never be false, and therefore cannot be defamatory. Of course, the line between a statement of fact and an opinion is often hard to draw, particularly in the area of literary or artistic criticism.

Not surprisingly, art, literary, and drama critics have frequently been accused of libel after they have published particularly scathing reviews. When criticizing the work of artists, the critic is free to use rhetorical hyperbole as long as the statements do not reflect on the character of the artist. For example, in the early seventies Gore Vidal sued William F. Buckley, Jr., for calling Vidal's book *Myra Breckenridge* pornography. The court held that, in context, the statement did not assail Vidal's character by suggesting that he himself was a pornographer. Thus the statement was not defamatory.

An example of criticism that did assail character is a famous case from the 1890s, in which the American artist James Whistler won a defamation suit against John Ruskin, the English art critic. In his assessment of Whistler's painting *Nocturne in Brown and Gold*, Ruskin wrote: "I have seen, and heard, much of Cockney impudence before now, but never expected to hear a coxcomb ask 200 guineas for flinging a pot of paint in the public's face." On the surface, this statement was an expression of opinion of the painting's worth. At the same time it implied facts about Whistler's motives, suggesting that he was defrauding the public by charging money for something that was not even art. The court found these implied facts to be defamatory since they described Whistler as unfit professionally.

If an opinion concerns a topic of public interest, it *might* be allowed, since such opinions do have some, if limited, privilege. Such a situation arose in *Lavin* v. *New York News, Inc.*, when a court declined to find that a photograph of two policemen captioned "Best Cops Money Can Buy" constituted defamation. The court held that the photograph and the accompanying article on organized crime came within the privilege concerning opinions on subjects of public interest.

Consent

Someone accused of defamation may also raise the defense of *consent*. It is not libelous to publish a photograph of a person who has consented to its publication. In this situation, the extent of the material that may be legally published is governed by the terms and context of the consent.

An interesting case that turned on what constitutes consent concerned a student humor magazine that had run a piece for Mother's Day consisting of four pictures. One picture was totally black. Under it was the legend "Father Loves Mother." Another picture showed a little girl with the caption "Daughter Loves Mother (And wants to be one too!)." A third picture showed a boy whose arm was tattooed with a heart enclosing the word *mother* captioned "Sailor Boy Loves Mother," and the final picture showed a face partly covered by a hood, labeled "Midwife Loves Mother." The picture of the little girl happened to be a photograph of the daughter of a local Methodist minister, a Mr. Langford, and it was rumored that he was about to sue the school newspaper for libel. Langford maintained that the pictures and captions made innuendos about the unchastity of his daughter, his wife, and himself. Another student newspaper sent two reporters to interview the minister, and he gladly consented to the interview. When the minister filed suit, the newspaper that had conducted the interview published an article which truthfully set out the facts of the suit and contained material from the interview. It also republished the allegedly libelous material. The minister then sued the second paper, but he lost because the court found that he had consented to republication of the material.

In 1991, the Supreme Court of Nebraska found that a model's consent to use her picture in connection with the sale of products shown on a brochure was a defense to her invasion of privacy and libel claim against the issuer of the brochure.

The court found that the brochure used for selling bathtubs and refrigerators did not libel the model who was shown on the cover wearing only a bathing towel, even though the cover also displayed the word "sex." When the brochure was fully opened, the letters forming the word became part of the phrase, "See us next time you build or buy." The remainder of the brochure did not suggest that the model was promoting or selling herself for another's sexual gratification, she was not identified, and the brochure did not disclose how she might be contacted.

Further, the court held that even if the brochure was libelous, the model's consent to her photograph being used in the brochure was an absolute defense. Although the model did not know exactly what uses might be made of her picture, she admitted that she could have restricted its use, but did not.

Reports of Official Proceedings

Another defense to what would otherwise be considered defamation is that the statement or picture was part of a report of official proceedings or a *public meeting*. As long as the context is a "fair and accurate" account of those proceedings, there can be no liability, even if the picture in question is both defamatory and false. Thus, a photograph depicting a witness testifying before a congressional panel and falsely captioned "Organized Crime Investigation" would not give rise to a claim by the witness. The requirement that the publication be fair and accurate means that whatever was published must be a fair and balanced rendition. For example, a writer may not quote only one side of an argument made in court if there was also a rebuttal to that argument. The account need not be an exact quote, and it is permissible to include some background material to put an accompanying photograph into proper perspective. However, a photographer or caption-writer must be careful not to include extraneous information such as editorial comments (which are themselves defamatory), because these will not be protected by the report of official proceedings defense.

Photographers and lawyers learned long ago that it is not always clear what constitutes an official proceeding or public meeting. Court proceedings from arrest to conviction are definitely official proceedings. On the other hand, photographs taken outside of court are not. A newsletter sent by a legislator to constituents does not generally constitute an official proceeding, whereas a political convention probably does.

Reply

Another defense to an accusation of libel is that of *reply*. If someone is defamed, that person is privileged to reply, even if the first person is defamed in the process. This privilege is limited to the extent that the reply may not exceed the provocation. For example, if A publishes a photograph of B and indicates that B is a communist, B has a right to reply that A is a liar or that A is a right-wing extremist, because either of these comments bears some relation to the original defamation. If, later on, A sues B for libel because of the statement about A being a right-wing extremist, B can simply show that the statement was in response to the material published by A: the reply defense. But if B made the mistake of responding by calling A a thief—a statement that bears no relation to A's accusation—B cannot have recourse to the reply defense.

Statute of Limitations

Another possible defense is the *statute of limitations*. Basically, statutes of limitations limit the time period within which an injured party can sue. The reason for these time limits is the difficulty of resolving old claims once the evidence becomes stale and the witnesses forget or disappear.

In the case of libel, the injured party must generally sue within one or two years from the date of first publication, although in some states the period is longer. If suit is brought after this time has elapsed, the statute of limitations will bar the suit.

For photographs, the period of time allowed by statutes of limitations for libel begins when a photograph is first published. Since publication means the act of communicating the matter at issue to one or more persons, the first publication of a book, magazine, or newspaper containing the photograph is deemed to occur when the publisher releases the finished product for sale. A second edition is generally not considered a separate publication for calculating time elapsed under the statute of limitations, at least where the single-publication rule is followed.

Absence of Actual Malice

The defense most frequently used in recent libel suits was created by the United States Supreme Court in 1964 in *New York Times Co. v. Sullivan*. The case against the *Times* concerned a photo advertisement it published which contained some inaccuracies and supposedly defamed L.B. Sullivan, the police chief of Montgomery, Alabama. The Supreme Court held that the *New York Times* was not guilty of libel, stating the existence of a profound national commitment to the principle that debate on public issues should be uninhibited, robust, and wide-open, and that it may well include vehement, caustic, and sometimes unpleasantly sharp attacks on government and public officials.

Thus the Court found that the First Amendment provides some protection to writings which criticize public officials for anything they do that is in any way relevant to their official conduct.

By virtue of the First Amendment protection, or privilege, when a public official sues for defamation the official must prove with "convincing clarity" that the defendant published the statement with "actual malice." Actual malice is defined as knowledge of the falsity, or a reckless disregard for the truth or falsity, of the statements published. Reckless disregard is further defined as serious doubts about the truth of the statement. Conflicts often arise in suits against newspapers when a public official is the plaintiff and tries to find the source of a paper's information in order to show reckless disregard of the truth, while the newspaper tries to protect its source.

The *Sullivan* case placed a greater burden of proof upon public officials in defamation suits. Prior to *Sullivan*, a preponderance of the evidence was simply proof of defamation, but now the courts require "convincing clarity," which is somewhere between the "preponderance of the evidence" required in most civil suits and the "proof beyond a reasonable doubt" required in criminal cases.

For the photographer, the result of *Sullivan* was the public-official privilege—the privilege to examine public officials with considerable scrutiny.

The standards resulting from *Sullivan* were applied in 1984 in the highly publicized case of *Sharon* v. *Time Inc.*, which arose after the massacre of Palestinian refugees by Lebanese Phalangists in retaliation for the assassination of Lebanon's President Gemayel. At the time, Lebanon was occupied by Israeli forces and Ariel Sharon was Israel's defense minister. *Time* magazine published a story alleging that Sharon had secretly discussed the possibility of such a retaliatory attack with Gemayel's family, who remained politically powerful. Sharon sued *Time*, which steadfastly refused to retract the allegations.

The jury held that *Time*'s article was false, and that Sharon was defamed by it. But the jury also found that *Time* did not possess actual malice, which meant that the magazine did not have to pay any damages. Both sides claimed victory. Sharon declared himself vindicated of the allegations, while *Time* pointed to the fact that it did not have to pay damages to Sharon. Most commentators, however, agreed that *Time* suffered great damage to its journalistic reputation.

Ariel Sharon went on to file a second lawsuit for libel against *Time* in Israel. According to a legal treaty between the United States and Israel, judgments of Israeli courts are recognized in America and vice versa. The Tel Aviv district court judge ruled that he would accept the American jury's ruling that *Time* had defamed Sharon and printed false material about him. Significantly, it is not necessary to prove malice in a libel suit under Israeli law; it is necessary only to show that a story is false and defamatory. Consequently, *Time*'s Israeli lawyer was reported as stating that the magazine had little chance of winning in the Israeli court.

In January of 1986, while the Tel Aviv judge was in the process of deciding the case, the parties announced an out-of-court settlement. In return for Ariel Sharon's dropping his libel action, *Time* stated to the Tel Aviv court that the reference to Sharon's supposed conversation in Beirut was "erroneous." In addition, *Time* agreed to pay part of the Israeli minister's legal fees. The *Time* statement appeared to acknowledge more culpability than had previously been admitted. The difference in the outcomes in the two cases illustrates the importance of requiring a plaintiff to prove actual malice in a libel suit. To some extent, this requirement in American law results in broader protection for the press than exists in other countries.

The American jury's verdict in *Sharon* may have spurred a settlement in another much-publicized case being tried at the same time, *Westmoreland* v. *CBS*. In *Westmoreland*, the former commander of American troops in Vietnam challenged allegations of wrong-doing on his part made by CBS in a documentary about the war.

It has been speculated that the parties in *Westmoreland* realized that a verdict similar to that in *Sharon* would be damaging to both of them. Settlement of the case allowed both sides to claim victory without the necessity of submitting the issues to the jury.

The depth of criticism required for a finding of libel under the public-official privilege created in *Sharon* varies from case to case. The most intimate aspects of private life are fair game when one is discussing an elected official or a candidate's qualifications for political office. On the other hand, when discussing civil servants such as police and firefighters, only comments directly related to their function as civil servants are similarly privileged.

The Supreme Court has defined public officials as those "who have, or appear to the public to have, substantial responsibility for or control over the conduct of governmental affairs." This category has been held to include all civil servants from police officers to secretaries. Recently, the Court has begun applying the public-official exception to public figures as well—but it has experienced a good deal of difficulty in determining who should be considered a public figure.

A Public Figure

At present the United States Supreme Court recognizes two ways in which people may become public figures. The first is to "occupy positions of such persuasive power and influence that they are deemed public figures for all purposes." This category includes those who are frequently in the news but are not public officials, such as Henry Kissinger, Bob Dylan, and Walter Cronkite. The fact that they are deemed public figures "for all purposes" means that the scope of privileged comment about them is virtually without limit.

The second way of becoming a public figure is to "thrust [oneself] to the forefront of particular public controversies in order to influence the resolution of the issues involved." This category has two requirements. First, there must be a public controversy. The Court in *Time, Inc.* v. *Firestone* held that not every newsworthy event is a public controversy. Nor is an event a public controversy merely because there may be different opinions as to the propriety of an act.

The *Firestone* case is a good example of how narrowly the Court applies the term "public controversy." *Time* magazine accidentally published a story stating that Mr. Firestone was divorced from Mrs. Firestone because of [his] "extreme cruelty and [their] adultery." In fact, the divorce was granted because the judge found that neither party to the divorce displayed "the least susceptibility to domestication," a novel ground for divorce under Florida law. *Time* went astray because the judge himself had once commented that there was enough testimony of extramarital adventures on both sides "to make Dr. Freud's hair curl." In its defense against Mrs. Firestone's suit for libel, *Time* insisted that Mrs. Firestone was a public figure. As evidence of this, it showed that the divorce had been covered in nearly every major newspaper and that Mrs. Firestone herself had held periodic press conferences during the trial. But the Court refused to equate a *cause célèbre* with a public controversy. As a result, Mrs. Firestone was required to prove only that *Time* had been negligent in its reading of the Court's opinion and that there was actual injury.

The second requirement in this public-figure category is that the person has voluntarily thrust himself or herself into the controversy in order to influence the issues. This requirement would be met if someone's actions were calculated to draw attention to that person or to arouse public sentiment, but not if the person were arrested or convicted. A student who makes a speech during a peace demonstration, say, is considered a public figure only with respect to the subject of the demonstration. In matters that have nothing to do with the political controversy, the courts would probably regard the student as a private individual.

To reiterate, the Supreme Court will require only public officials and public figures to prove actual malice in a defamation suit. Yet even private persons may have to prove negligence if they sue a newspaper for libel which occurred in a piece relating to a matter of public concern. Although the Supreme Court held that the plaintiff in *Firestone* did not have the heavy burden of proof of a public figure, she still had to prove negligence in her suit for libel. This is more difficult than that what is required of the average person who has been defamed in regard to some private, unnewsworthy matter. Generally, the everyday, private person who sues for libel does not need to prove actual malice or any other state of mind. All he or she need demonstrate to the court is that a writing, or a photo caption, identifying him or her conveyed a defamatory meaning and was published.

The Supreme Court recently increased the burden of proof for private plaintiffs suing newspapers writing matters of public concern. In *Philadelphia Newspapers, Inc.* v. *Hepps*, a 1986 case, a businessman operating a franchise in Philadelphia sued the *Philadelphia Inquirer* for publication of several articles asserting that he had links to organized crime and had used these links to influence local government. The Court held that in such a case the plaintiff, Hepps, not the defendant, will bear the burden of proof on the issue of the truth or falsity of the statement. The Court found that the Constitution requires that the burden be so shifted in order to ensure that true speech on matters of public concern not be stifled.

Court opinions seem to indicate that a private person suing a newspaper on a matter of public concern will have to prove both that there was negligence on the part of the paper, and that the information published was in fact false. How does one determine whether the information involved is of public concern? The distinction may hinge on whether or not the defendant represents the media. The Supreme Court dealt with the media-nonmedia distinction in a case involving a reporting service that published and circulated a grossly inaccurate credit report. The reporting service pleaded First Amendment protection, but the Court, by a five-to-four vote, held that since the credit report was not a matter of public concern, it was not entitled to protection by the First Amendment. Thus, the injured business had only to prove defamation and publication.

Unfortunately, the Court did not define what kind of speech or photograph *is* of public concern. Lacking such a definition, news writers and photojournalists need to be extremely careful about the subjects of their reports and pictures.

A question that has often been raised by legal scholars, but has as yet not received an answer from the courts, is whether a person who at one time was a public figure or involved in a matter of public concern can ever effectively return to private life. It is probably better to remain on the safe side and treat anyone who has been out of the lime-light for more than five years as a private person.

Despite the tremendous burden of proof placed upon public officials and public figures, they are still able to win in many defamation suits. For example, Barry Goldwater was successful in his suit against Ralph Ginzburg, who had published an article which stated that Goldwater was psychotic and therefore unfit to be president. Goldwater proved that material in the article was intentionally distorted. In a later case, actress Carol Burnett won a libel suit against the *National Enquirer*. The article said that Burnett had been drunk and boisterous in a Wash-ington restaurant when in fact her behavior had been beyond reproach. Burnett was able to show that the article was published with reckless disregard for the truth or falsity of the facts and thus satisfied the mal-ice requirement.

Protection Against Defamation Suits

Since the law on libel is complicated, and subject to continual modifi-cation by the Supreme Court, any potentially libelous work should be submitted to a lawyer before publication is considered. Remember, everyone directly involved in the publication of libelous material can be held liable. Photographers should be aware that publishers may at-tempt to protect themselves from defamation suits by including a clause in the photographer's contract stating that the photographer guarantees not to have libeled anyone and accepts responsibility for covering costs if the publisher is sued. The risks involved in agreeing to such a clause are obvious. It is also wise to obtain a signed privacy and property release form from anyone whose name or work is being associated with yours. See the end of chapter 3 for sample release forms.

THE RIGHT
OF PRIVACY

The right to be protected from a wrongful invasion of privacy, largely taken for granted today, is a relatively new legal concept. In fact, the right of privacy was not suggested as a legal principle until 1890, when arguments for developing the right appeared in a *Harvard Law Review* article written by the late Justice Louis Brandeis and his law partner, Samuel Warren. This article, written largely because of excessive media attention given to the social affairs of Warren's wife, maintained that the media were persistently "overstepping in every direction the obvious bounds of propriety and of decency" in violation of the individual's right "to be let alone."

From this rather modest beginning the concept of a right to privacy began to take hold. In many of the early privacy cases the *Harvard Law Review* article was cited as justification for upholding privacy claims, although courts also found their own justifications. For example, in 1905 a Georgia court suggested that the right of privacy is rooted in natural law. In the words of the court: "The right of privacy has its foundations in the instincts of nature. It is recognized intuitively, consciousness being the witness that can be called to establish its existence." Other courts have upheld right-of-privacy laws on constitutional grounds, both state and federal, arguing that although there is no express recognition of a right to privacy in the U.S. Constitution, it can nevertheless be inferred from the combined language of the First, Fourth, Fifth, Ninth, and Fourteenth Amendments.

Although the right of privacy is now generally recognized, the precise nature of the right varies from state to state. Some states, such as New York, Oklahoma, Utah, Virginia, and California, have enacted right-of-privacy statutes. Others simply recognize the right as a matter of common law. Others—Texas, Nebraska, Rhode Island, and Wisconsin—expressly refuse to recognize a right of privacy, while still others have not yet taken a position. Because the right of privacy is not consistent throughout the states, you should keep in mind that the situations discussed in this chapter might be handled differently in the state where you live or work. The cases here should not be relied upon to determine a photographer's rights and liabilities. They are included simply to illustrate some of the legal developments in the area of privacy rights so that you can avoid obvious traps, identify problems as they arise, and know when to consult a lawyer. Since most photographers distribute their work throughout the country, it is prudent to comply with the most stringent state requirements.

Some of the confusion surrounding the right of privacy can be resolved by dividing the right of privacy into four specific categories: (1) intrusion upon another's seclusion, (2) public disclosure of private facts, (3) portrayal of another in a false light, and (4) commercial appropriation of another's name or likeness. These categories represent the four different types of civil invasion of privacy currently recognized by the courts.

Intrusion upon Another's Seclusion

At issue in intrusion upon another's seclusion is the extent to which a photographer intrudes upon someone's right of privacy for purposes of taking pictures to be used in combination with political, personal, or biographical commentary. An intrusion upon another's seclusion will be wrongful if three elements are present. First, there must be an actual intrusion of some sort. Second, the intrusion must be of a type that would be offensive to a reasonable person; courts will not consider the particular sensibilities of the plaintiff. Third, the intruder must have entered that which is considered someone's private domain. Thus, for example, it is generally not unlawful to take pictures of a person in a public place or disclose facts the person has discussed publicly. It is likely, however, that an intrusion would be wrongful if someone goes on someone else's land without permission or opens someone else's private desk and reads materials found there. Publication is not a necessary element in a case for intrusion since the intrusion itself is the invasion of privacy.

The nature of a wrongful intrusion upon another's seclusion is well illustrated by two cases: *Dietemann* v. *Time, Inc.* and *Galella* v. *Onassis*. In *Dietemann*, the plaintiff claimed to be a healer. Investigators for *Life* magazine sought to prove that he was in fact a charlatan. In the process of checking out his claim, reporters entered Dieteman's house under false pretenses, and while in his house they surreptitiously took pictures and recorded conversations. This information was then written up in an exposé appearing in *Life*. The court held that the healer's right of privacy had indeed been violated, since there was no question that his seclusion was invaded unreasonably.

An even more obvious intrusion is illustrated by *Galella* v. *Onassis*. Ronald Galella is a freelance photographer specializing in photographs of celebrities, who is tenacious and persistent. For a number of years Jacqueline Onassis, Caroline Kennedy, John Kennedy, Jr., and other members of the Kennedy family were among his favorite subjects. Onassis and the others were constantly confronted by Galella, who used highly offensive chase scene techniques, in parks and churches, at funeral services, theatres, schools, and elsewhere in order to obtain photographs. One of his practices was to shock or startle his subjects in order to photograph them in a state of surprise. While taking these photographs, he would sometimes utter offensive or snide comments. After hearing a wealth of evidence regarding this type of behavior, the court, in a scathing opinion, held that Galella had wrongfully intruded upon the seclusion of his subjects. Finding monetary damages to be an inadequate remedy, the court issued a permanent injunction that prohibited Galella from getting within a certain distance of Onassis and the others. A decade later, the court found that Galella had repeatedly violated this injunction and was thus guilty of civil contempt. In order to avoid a prison sentence of up to six years and a fine of up to $120,000, Galella promised the court he would never again photograph Onassis or her children.

In both *Dietemann* and *Galella* the defendants maintained that any attempt to restrain their efforts to get information or photographs was constitutionally suspect, since it would infringe upon their First Amendment rights. These arguments are not particularly persuasive. Courts have universally attempted to *balance* rights in intrusion cases: The right of the press to obtain information is balanced against the equal right of the individual to enjoy privacy and seclusion. Thus, the courts have refused to construe the First Amendment as a license to steal, trespass, harass, or engage in any other conduct that would clearly be wrongful or offensive.

This balancing approach is apparent in *Galella*. The court found that the intrusions were so pervasive and offensive that it did not matter that many of the acts occurred while Onassis and her children were in public rather than private places. Their right to privacy had been significantly infringed. Furthermore, the products of Galella's efforts were trivial, being nothing more than fodder for gossip magazines. Thus, the harmful effect of suppressing his First Amendment freedoms was found to be slight or nonexistent. Significantly, the court did not forbid further photographs, but merely regulated the manner in which they could be taken.

For the dedicated photojournalist, the possibility of an intrusion suit should always be weighed against the natural tendency to aggressively pursue the facts, but even photojournalists on important assignments have no right to harass, trespass, use electronic surveillance, or enter a private domain.

Photographers should be aware that even a photograph taken in a public place can result in liability for wrongful intrusion. In *Daily Times Democrat* v. *Graham*, the court found wrongful intrusion when a photographer took the picture of an obese woman whose skirt was blown upward while she was standing in a fun house. Photographers should also be aware that some states have statutes that make the use of hidden cameras a misdemeanor.

Public Disclosure of Private Facts

The public disclosure of private facts was the aspect of the right of privacy that first prompted Warren and Brandeis to publish their article in the *Harvard Law Review*. Plaintiffs are less likely to win in these circumstances, however, because the First Amendment protection that modern courts apply to "newsworthy information," which includes educational or informative material, as well as current events, makes it unlikely that photographers depicting matters of public interest will incur liability for public disclosure. Where the information disclosed is true, the First Amendment freedoms afforded to the press almost invariably outweigh an individual's right of privacy. Only in very limited circumstances will the balance be shifted in favor of the individual.

In order to bring a case for this kind of invasion of privacy, the plaintiff must prove that private facts about him or her were publicly disclosed and that the disclosure would be objectionable to a person of ordinary sensibilities.

The first question, then, is whether a photograph involves private facts. This is basically a matter of common sense; anything that one keeps to oneself and would obviously not wish to be made public is probably a private fact. Thus, private debts, criminal records, certain diseases, psychological problems, and the like usually involve private facts.

There is some seemingly private information which courts will treat as public. For purposes of defining potential invasion of privacy liability, "official public records" include legislative, judicial, and executive records and records of documents affecting title to property, such as deeds and vehicle title transfers. Therefore, information contained in a public record is never considered to be private. This principle was firmly established by the Supreme Court in the mid-seventies in *Cox Broadcasting Corp.* v. *Cohn.* At issue was the constitutionality of a Georgia statute which made it a misdemeanor to publicly disclose the identity of a rape victim. In violation of this statute, someone at the broadcasting company made known the name of a rape victim, based upon information gleaned from a court indictment. The plaintiff, the father of the deceased victim, sued the broadcaster for publicly disclosing private facts, arguing that the statute converted the information into private facts. The highest Georgia court ruled in favor of the father, but when the case reached the Supreme Court, the decision was reversed. In a sweeping opinion, the Court declared that no one could be liable for truthfully disclosing information contained in an official court record, or, by implication, any other public record. Such disclosures enjoy an "absolute privilege" and are treated as public facts, regardless of how personal the information may be. An absolute privilege also exists for public disclosure of private facts made in the context of judicial, legislative, or executive proceedings.

The second requirement a plaintiff must meet in a case for public disclosure is proving that the public disclosure of private facts would be offensive to a reasonable person of ordinary sensibilities. Although a recluse may place a very high premium on absolute privacy, the law does not give such special rights. If a disclosure is minimal and therefore not offensive to the sensibilities of reasonable persons, the recluse will have no cause of action even though, from a recluse's personal perspective, the disclosure may seem egregious.

Disclosures of newsworthy information are generally protected by the First Amendment. As long as such disclosure is truthful, the disclosure is privileged, and an individual's right to privacy will outweigh First Amendment freedoms only when the disclosure is outrageous in the extreme. This privilege regarding newsworthy information significantly insulates media photographers from liability for invasion of privacy.

Photographs with seemingly private subject matter tend to be treated as public if the photographs were taken in public places. For example, in *Anderson* v. *Fisher Broadcasting Companies, Inc.*, the Oregon Supreme Court refused to recognize an accident victim's claims that his privacy was invaded by a tape shown in an ad for a news feature on emergency medical care. The court held that unless the plaintiff could prove fraud or intentional infliction of emotional distress, there was no liability even though the facts contained on the tape were not newsworthy. Similarly, courts have ruled that neither a photograph of a couple embracing in a marketplace nor a photograph of a defendant in a courtroom were actionable.

Generally, truthful disclosures pertaining to public figures or public officials are considered newsworthy, at least to the extent that the disclosure bears some reasonable relationship to the public role. If, however, the disclosure is highly personal, such as sexual habits, and has no bearing upon the individual's public role, the disclosure may not be privileged and thus may be actionable. This is particularly true where the individual does not enjoy a great deal of fame or notoriety. A presidential candidate or a mass murderer, for example, could expect considerably greater intrusions into and disclosure of his or her private affairs than a minor public official or a one-time traffic offender. Similarly, private individuals who are involuntarily thrust into the public light will receive more protection than those who seek fame and notoriety.

A person no longer in the public eye may or may not be considered newsworthy. Some people, of course, remain newsworthy even though they have long since left the public eye, but generally, the newsworthiness of people who once were public officials or public figures tends to decrease with the passage of time. To the extent that these people become less newsworthy, their right to privacy becomes stronger.

Melvin v. *Reid*, decided in 1931, illustrates the point. The plaintiff in this case was a former prostitute who had been charged with murder but was acquitted after a rather sensational trial. Thereafter, she led a conventional life; she married and made new friends who were unaware of her sordid past. Some years after the trial, a movie of the woman's early life was made, in which she was identified by her maiden name. She sued, alleging public disclosure of private facts, and the court ruled in her favor. The court conceded that the events that initially brought the woman into the public eye remained newsworthy, but stated that to identify her by name constituted a "willful and wanton disregard of the charity which should actuate us in our social intercourse." The moviemakers' disclosure was deemed so outrageous that it could not be considered newsworthy and the disclosure privilege therefore did not apply.

The case of *Briscoe* v. *Reader's Digest Association, Inc.* provides an interesting contrast. In this 1971 case, the Reader's Digest had published an article about truck hijacking. The article related a hijack attempt involving the plaintiff, Briscoe, who was identified by name. During the years between the hijack attempt and the defendant's disclosure, Briscoe had led an exemplary life. He sued for public disclosure of private facts, alleging that as a result of the article he had been shunned and abandoned by his daughter and friends, who previously had not known of the incident.

Although the facts of *Briscoe* were very similar to those of *Melvin*, and although the issue of outrageous disclosure was raised, the information in the *Briscoe* case was considered newsworthy and thus privileged. That this disclosure was considered newsworthy, whereas the disclosure in the *Melvin* case was not, might best be explained by the fact that the Melvin disclosure intruded upon the sex life of the plaintiff, revealing that she had once been a prostitute. It would appear that a disclosure is most likely to be considered unconscionable, and thus not newsworthy, if it relates to someone's sexuality, which is perhaps the most private aspect of anyone's life.

It should be observed that the *social mores* or *outrageous disclosure* test applies only where the plaintiff is in some way newsworthy. A public disclosure involving an ordinary person who is not newsworthy will be actionable if it is merely offensive to the sensibilities of reasonable persons. So, the question is really one of degree.

One final question that has been the subject of litigation in this area is whether an excerpt taken from a publication and used in an advertisement is privileged to the same extent as it is in the original publication. Although the answer is not altogether clear, it appears to depend on whether the advertisement is used to promote the work from which the excerpt was taken or to promote something else.

In *Friedan* v. *Friedan*, the defendant, Betty Friedan, the noted feminist, wrote and published an account of her early domestic life. She included several photographs of those early years, one of which was a family portrait of her, her former husband, and their child. This picture was selected for use in a television commercial promoting the defendant's publication. Carl Friedan, the defendant's former husband, sued her, alleging that the original publication, as well as the advertisements, constituted an invasion of his privacy as a public disclosure of private facts.

The court easily disposed of Carl Friedan's case. Since Betty Friedan was a noted feminist, her life was a matter of public interest. By virtue of being her former spouse, Carl Friedan also became newsworthy, despite the fact that he had persistently sought to avoid publicity. Because he was deemed newsworthy, the public disclosure about his past private life was permissible. As to the commercial, the court held that where an advertisement is used to promote the publication from which the excerpt was taken, the advertisement will enjoy the same protection as the original publication. Since Betty Friedan's biographical account was permissible, the television commercial was also permissible.

The case of *Rinaldi* v. *Village Voice, Inc.* involved a slightly different situation. The plaintiff was a prominent judge. The *Village Voice* published an article critical of his performance on the bench. There was no question as to whether the article was permissible, since the plaintiff was clearly newsworthy and the disclosure pertained to his public role. At issue was the question of whether the *Village Voice* could incorporate excerpts from that article into an advertisement for itself. The court held that the advertisement was not permissible since the excerpts were used for the purpose of increasing subscriptions for subsequent issues of the newspaper. The *Village Voice* was held liable for public disclosure of private facts. Had the advertisement been used to promote the particular issue from which the excerpts were taken, it would, presumably, have been permissible under the reasoning applied in *Friedan*.

Where excerpts or photographs are used for purposes other than advertising, such as the circulation of galley proofs of forthcoming books to newspapers and magazines for review, the excerpts or photographs are more likely to enjoy the same privilege as information published in complete form. In *Estate of Hemingway* v. *Random House, Inc.*, Ernest Hemingway's widow brought an action against the writer and publisher of the book *Papa Hemingway*. The author had drawn largely on his own recollections of conversations with Ernest Hemingway, and included two chapters on the famous novelist's illness and death. The court found that Hemingway was clearly a public figure and rejected the widow's argument that the description of her feelings and conduct during the time of her husband's mental illness was so intimate and unwarranted as to constitute outrageous disclosure. The court also rejected her claim that even if disclosures in the book were protected by the First Amendment, circulation of galley proofs to book reviewers of sixteen journals and newspapers amounted to unlawful use of private facts for advertising purposes. In holding that circulation of proofs to reviewers is not generally advertisement, the court stated:

> A publisher, in circulating a book for review, risks unfavorable comment as well as praise; he places the work in the arena of debate. The same reasons which support the author's freedom to write and publish books require a similar freedom for their circulation, before publication, for comment by reviewers.

In summary, a public disclosure of private facts will support a lawsuit if the effect of the disclosure would be objectionable to persons of ordinary sensibilities, unless the disclosure is newsworthy. Whether a disclosure is or is not newsworthy will depend upon the social value of the facts disclosed, the extent to which the plaintiff voluntarily assumed public fame or notoriety, and the extent to which the disclosure related to the plaintiff's public role. Finally, even a disclosure relating to newsworthy persons may be actionable if it would outrage reasonable persons.

Portrayal of Another in a False Light

Portrayal of another in a false light has been actionable as an invasion of privacy for some time. In 1816, in what was probably the first case to address the issue, the poet Lord Byron successfully enjoined the publication under his name of a rather bad poem which he did not in fact write. Byron was extremely protective of his reputation and apparently felt that the inferior piece would harm his image as an artist.

To bring a suit for false light, a plaintiff must prove that the defendant publicly portrayed the plaintiff in a false light and that the portrayal would be offensive to reasonable people had the damage been done to them. In cases involving the media, the plaintiff must also prove that the portrayal was done with malice.

Thus, false-light cases often involve works that falsely ascribe to the plaintiff particular conduct or action. Usually, photographs do not portray their subjects in a false light, but the accompanying caption or story may, in conjunction with the photograph, create a false impression. For instance, a caption which suggested that two nude models who were photographed together were lesbians was found to be a false-light invasion of privacy in *Douglass* v. *Hustler Magazine, Inc.*

Leverton v. *Curtis Publishing Co.* is another example. A young girl who had been struck by an automobile was photographed while a bystander lifted her to her feet, and that photograph appeared in a local newspaper the following day. Nearly two years later the *Saturday Evening Post* published an article entitled "They Ask to Be Killed," the gist of which was that most pedestrian injuries are the result of carelessness on the part of the pedestrian. The photograph of the girl was used to illustrate the story. The girl sued the *Post* for invasion of privacy, alleging among other things that the *Post* had portrayed her in a false light. The court ruled in her favor because the rational inference from the use of the photograph in the article was that the plaintiff had been injured because of her carelessness, when in fact she had been completely without fault. Thus, the *Post*'s portrayal of the accident victim as having engaged in careless conduct was essentially false.

A frequent cause of false-light cases involves publications that attribute to someone views or opinions that the person does not actually hold or statements that the person did not make.

An extreme case is *Spahn* v. *Julian Messner, Inc.* in which the defendant published a biography of Warren Spahn, a renowned baseball player. This biography was replete with fictionalized events, dramatizations, distorted chronologies, and fictionalized dialogues. Although the biography tended to glorify Spahn, it nevertheless placed him in a false, albeit radiant, light. As a result, the publisher was held liable for invasion of privacy.

Between the extreme in *Spahn* and a situation where the errors are irrelevant and minimal, it is difficult to predict where liability will lie. Distortions or inaccuracies involving insignificant events, places, and dates are likely to be safe, provided the errors are not pervasive. However, false statements pertaining to significant aspects of someone's life are more likely to result in liability, particularly if they involve highly personal and sensitive matters. The crucial question is whether the false portrayal would be offensive to a reasonable person in the position of the person portrayed. Was the plaintiff, as a result of the publication, humiliated, estranged from friends or family, or embarrassed?

False Light and Defamation: Similarities and Differences

In addition to proving an objectionable portrayal in a false-light case, the plaintiff might also have to prove malice—as is necessary in defamation. Defamation and false-light invasion of privacy have much in common, so that as the law evolves with respect to one, the other is also affected. In 1964, the Supreme Court in *New York Times Co.* v. *Sullivan* articulated a new requirement for liability in defamation cases: Where the plaintiff is a public figure, public official, or otherwise newsworthy, and where the defendant is a member of the media, the plaintiff must prove that the allegedly defamatory statement was made with malice. Malice is shown if the defendant knew the statement was false or published the statement with reckless disregard for its truth or falsity. The Court felt that an unreasonable limitation on First Amendment freedoms would result if liability was imposed for mere negligence or failure to use due care in ascertaining truth or falsity.

The *New York Times* rule was at first limited to defamation cases. It thus was fairly easy for a newsworthy plaintiff to avoid the more stringent proof-of-malice requirement by couching the complaint in terms of invasion of privacy rather than defamation. If a suit for invasion of privacy could be maintained, the plaintiff could prevail over the media defendant by simply proving negligence.

This rather obvious means of circumventing the *New York Times* rule was done away with three years later in *Time, Inc* v. *Hill*. The Supreme Court took the opportunity to extend the rationale of *New York Times* to false-light cases of invasion of privacy. A few years earlier, a family named Hill had been held hostage by escaped convicts, and the incident was subsequently portrayed in a play which differed in many material respects from the actual incident. After the play was written, *Life* magazine published a story on the incident which identified the Hills by name and stated as fact some of the fictionalized and dramatized parts of the play. In the Hills' suit, the Court required proof of malice even though the action was for invasion of privacy rather than defamation. As a result, newsworthy plaintiffs suing media defendants either for defamation or for invasion of privacy based upon public portrayal in a false light must prove that the defendant published with malice.

Although defamation and false-light cases are substantially similar, they do differ in three respects. First, the nature of the injury is different. Defamation is injury to the plaintiff's reputation within the community. False light is more inclusive, extending to injuries to the plaintiff's sensibilities caused by personal embarrassment, humiliation, estrangement of loved ones, and the like. Second, truth is an absolute defense for defamation, whereas it may not be for a false-light claim. This is because statements that might in fact be true or photographs that might be accurate may be published out of context so that the plaintiff is nevertheless presented in a false light. Finally, in defamation cases where the plaintiff is a private person who, by circumstances beyond his or her control, is thrust into the public eye, media defendants will be held liable for mere negligence, rather than malice. But in false-light cases, all newsworthy plaintiffs, whether or not they have voluntarily assumed their public role, must prove malice on the part of a media defendant.

Commercial Appropriation of Another's Name or Likeness

Commercial appropriation of someone's name or likeness as an invasion of privacy bears little resemblance to cases based upon wrongful intrusion, public disclosure of private facts, or portrayal in a false light. In all of those situations, the plaintiff must prove that the defendant's words or pictures caused the plaintiff to suffer humiliation, embarrassment, or loss of self-esteem, focusing on the injury to the plaintiff's sensibilities. In contrast, the law against appropriation is designed to protect someone's privately-owned or commercial interest in one's own name or likeness. Athletes, movie stars, authors, and other celebrities obviously receive a considerable amount of their income from the controlled exploitation of their names or likenesses. The monetary benefits from such exploitation would be minimal without some legal protection.

In order to bring a suit for this type of invasion of privacy, one need only prove that the defendant wrongfully appropriated the plaintiff's name or likeness for commercial purposes. "Appropriation" in this sense means use. The fact of appropriation is rarely at issue in these cases, since the use will be obvious. However, the purpose of the use must be commercial, or expected to bring profits, either directly or indirectly. A purely private use will not result in liability for wrongful appropriation.

As with the other kinds of invasion of privacy, any use that is considered newsworthy or informative will not be actionable as a commercial appropriation, even though some commercial gain might result from the use. As you might suspect, it is often difficult for a photographer to know where to draw the line between "trade and advertising" and "newsworthiness." Each case is looked at in light of its own facts, and often there are gray areas.

In 1990, the New York Court of Appeals concluded that a "real relationship" existed between a magazine article about in vitro fertilization and an accompanying photograph of an unidentified large family. The photograph, therefore, was newsworthy. The family had not given *Omni Magazine* permission to use their photograph and sued for invasion of privacy. The court stated that questions of newsworthiness "are better left to reasonable editorial judgment and discretion." Only where there is not any real relationship between a photograph and an article, or where the article is an "advertisement in disguise," should the judiciary intervene.

Namath v. *Sports Illustrated* involved the use of a celebrity's likeness in an advertisement. *Sports Illustrated* published an article about the 1969 Super Bowl game that included some photographs of Joe Namath. One of those photographs was subsequently used in an advertisement promoting the magazine. Namath sued, alleging that the use of his photograph was a wrongful commercial appropriation. The court held for the magazine, maintaining that its use of Namath's picture was primarily informative because it indicated the general content and nature of the magazine as well as what subscribers could expect to receive in the future. Commercial benefits were only incidental. However, if *Sports Illustrated* had used Namath's picture in such a way that it appeared that Namath endorsed the magazine, the use would have been actionable, since the commercial purpose could not be said to be incidental to the dissemination of information.

In *Booth* v. *Curtis Publishing Co.*, Holiday magazine shot and published a photograph of actress Shirley Booth as part of a news story about a resort. Miss Booth consented to this use of her photograph but brought suit when Holiday republished her photograph six months later as part of an advertisement for *Holiday* subscriptions. Here, too, the court denied relief, holding that *Holiday*'s use of the photograph fell within the special exemption for incidental advertising of a news medium itself. The court also noted that the actress was properly and fairly presented. The court reasoned that the magazine used the photographs solely to illustrate the quality and content of the magazine and that, therefore, the use of the photographs was incidental.

Clearly, use of someone's name or likeness in solicitation or advertisement may not be actionable if the use is newsworthy or if the advertising is incidental to informational purposes.

A commercial misappropriation, as well as false-light invasion of privacy, was found in *Douglass* v. *Hustler Magazine, Inc.*, which concerned photographs published in Hustler. The pictures had been taken with the model's consent, but she understood that they would appear in *Playboy*. The court found that model-actress Robin Douglass's right to publicize herself was undermined when *Hustler* deprived her of the choice of publications in which her pictures would appear. However, the court found that *Hustler*'s publication of stills from a movie in which Douglass appeared was not misappropriation because the still photographs were in the public domain and, therefore, beyond Douglass's control.

Right of Publicity

In suing for unauthorized commercial appropriation, a person is exercising the *right of publicity*, which is defined as a person's right to exploit his or her name, likeness, or reputation and is commonly applied to entertainers and other famous people. In one case, the right of publicity was held to be limited by certain aspects of the federal copyright law. In *Baltimore Orioles* v. *Major League Baseball Players*, baseball players sued club owners, asserting that their performances during ball games were being telecast without the players' consent and that under state law, the telecasting constituted a misappropriation of the players' property right of publicity in their performances. The court found that the players' performance was within the scope of their employment and thus the club owners owned the copyright to the performance. When state and federal law conflict, the federal law takes precedence. In this case, the players' rights of publicity in the game-time performances, as granted by state law, were found to be preempted by federal copyright law.

Appropriation after a Celebrity's Death

A final question is whether a lawsuit based upon commercial appropriation can be brought after the death of the person whose name or likeness was used. There is considerable controversy over this issue.

In a 1984 case in New York, the court denied the defendants the right to name their theatre after playwright Tennessee Williams without his estate's consent. The court held that New York recognizes a common-law right of publicity, and ruled that the right of publicity survives death and descends to the deceased's heirs.

In a similar case involving the Elvis Presley estate, the plaintiff, Factors Etc., Inc., had acquired the exclusive right to market the name and likeness of Elvis Presley during Presley's lifetime. The issue was whether the license remained effective after Presley's death.

Factors Etc. sued, after Presley's death, to prevent another company from distributing posters bearing Presley's image. The federal court, sitting in New York and applying New York law, ruled in favor of Factors, holding that when a party has the right to exploit a name or likeness during the lifetime of the subject, the right survives that person's death.

In another case involving the same license and essentially the same facts, but decided in the state of Tennessee under Tennessee law, the court reached the opposite opinion. The Memphis Development Foundation had solicited money from the public for purposes of erecting a statue of Presley. A donation of twenty-five dollars or more entitled the contributor to an eight-inch pewter replica of the statue. The foundation sought a court ruling on whether the exclusive license of Factors Etc., Inc. to Presley's likeness was still valid. This time the court held that a suit based upon commercial appropriation will under no circumstances survive the death of the person portrayed.

Since then the Tennessee legislature has passed a statute which explicitly states that the right to publicity *will* survive death and pass to the heir of the person whose name or likeness is commercially appropriated for a period of ten years after the person's death. Several other states, including California, Florida, Oklahoma, and Virginia, have passed similar laws. Such statutes guarantee the survival of such a right regardless of whether the person's name was commercially exploited during life. However, some states, while recognizing that the right to publicity can survive death, maintain that it will do so only if it was commercially exploited during life. This raises a difficult question because it gives no rights to the heirs of those famous individuals who chose not to exploit their names and faces while alive. Nevertheless, in *Martin Luther King Jr. Center For Social Change, Inc.* v. *American Heritage*, Coretta Scott King persuaded the court to enjoin American Heritage from selling plastic busts of Dr. King even though Dr. King had not commercially exploited his fame during life.

Since the law is unsettled on whether the right to sue for commercial appropriation survives death, it is difficult to make a general statement about the scope of such a right. Perhaps the most that can be said currently is that more and more courts and legislatures are recognizing that death should not automatically extinguish a right as meaningful and valuable as the right to control the use of a person's name or likeness. Many legal commentators approve this trend. Prudent photographers will attempt to comply with the strictest state laws since their work is likely to be distributed throughout the country.

Releases

Use of a photograph without written consent always raises the possibility of a lawsuit based on violation of some aspect of right to privacy. The surest and simplest way to avoid right-to-privacy suits is to obtain a release from the subject of the picture, or a release from the owner of any property photographed. (See the sample forms at the end of this chapter.)

In some states, such as New York, a photographer must obtain written consent for the use of a person's photograph in advertising or promotion. Although an oral release may be legally valid, it may also be difficult to enforce. Therefore, a release should be in writing. Be sure to specify, however, any limitations you want on use.

In *Cory* v. *Nintendo of America, Inc.*, a 1990 New York case, the court held that a model was barred from claiming an advertising agency's use of his photographs was a violation of his right of privacy, because the photographer's agent, who was authorized to sell the model's pictures, had signed a release with the advertising agent. The court stated that the advertising agency had no way of knowing any limitations on the agent's authority or any other reason to question the validity of the releases.

Generally, contracts require consideration—something that indicates compensation for a service rendered. As a release might be considered a contract, it is probably wise to pay the subject at least a small amount. However, one authority has stated that photographic releases are valid even when the photographer pays the subject nothing in modeling fees or use rights.

Most form releases are designed to protect the photographer. However, if a model has been hired by an advertising agency, the release should also cover the agency and the agency's client. A release should be drafted to include permission for the photographer to take the picture and permission for the photographer to make a certain use of the picture.

Sometimes litigation is threatened even with a release, as was the case with Vanessa Williams. In 1986, the former Miss America dropped a $400 million lawsuit against *Penthouse* magazine and two photographers, after concluding that she had signed a model release for the nude pictures which resulted in her relinquishing her crown under pressure.

It is common for a photographer to use a standard release form; however, this form should be used intelligently and modified as needed. Each release should specifically, if briefly, describe the subject matter and the use the photographer plans to make of the picture. A photographer would be wise to stamp the photograph with the same date as the date on the release form; this prevents any confusion or ambiguity as to what is covered when the photograph is released.

The protection of a release is no greater than the use the subject intends to grant. In *Buller* v. *Pulitzer Pub. Co.*, the court pointed out that, while a valid release waives the subject's right to sue for invasion of privacy, the burden of proof is upon the photographer to show just what was consented to. In *Russell* v. *Marboro Books*, a fashion model posed reading in bed, fully clothed, for an advertisement to promote a book club. The model signed a broadly-worded waiver that allowed the book club to make unrestricted use of the photograph, although it did not permit the photo to be altered. However, when the book company sold the photograph to a bed sheet manufacturer who retouched the photo, putting the title of a well-known pornographic book on the book the model held in the picture and running the photo with sexually suggestive copy, the model sued, alleging that her personal and professional standing were damaged by the bed sheet ad. The court awarded her damages based on invasion of privacy and libel, reasoning that the release was ineffective because the content of the photograph was altered so as to make it substantially unlike the original. Thus, a release should include a clause granting the right to alter a photograph and granting the right to add any type of copy or captions.

In the event a photographer has not obtained a release on a particular photograph, he may achieve limited protection against a third party's unauthorized use of the photograph by stating on the back of the picture: "This photograph cannot be altered for commercial or advertising use nor can it be copied, televised or reproduced in any form without the photographer's permission."

Photographers should be aware that a release signed by the parent of a child subject may not in all instances be valid. Current court decisions uphold the validity of releases signed by parents; however, language in these cases indicates that courts would refuse to find the releases binding in certain circumstances.

In *Faloona* v. *Hustler Magazine, Inc.*, the mother of two minor children executed a full release to a photographer for the use of nude photographs of her children. The children and their mother sued the photographer when the children's picture appeared in *Hustler* magazine. While not objecting to the photographs, per se, the plaintiffs believed that publication in *Hustler* constituted false-light invasion of privacy, public disclosure of private facts, and commercial misappropriation. The court applied Texas law, which provides that a parent has the authority to consent to matters of substantial legal significance concerning a child, and dismissed the case. New York and California have laws similar to those of Texas on the issue of parental consent; presumably, similar cases would have the same outcome in these jurisdictions. However, in *Faloona*, *Hustler* showed the children's photo to illustrate a review of a sex education book in which the photo originally appeared. Had *Hustler* used the photo in a salacious manner, the court probably would have invalidated the consent.

In *Shields* v. *Gross*, the court held that when the parent or guardian of a minor gives unrestricted consent to a photographer to make a commercial use of the minor's photograph, the minor may not later on make use of the common-law right to break a contract entered into while she was a minor. However, photographers should be aware that this case contains a strong dissent and the holding was influenced by the fact Ms. Shields was a professional actress, although a child. The holding has evoked critical commentary, as many believe that a minor's right to privacy should supersede the business community's interest in binding minors to contractual terms. The law may change in the future to reflect this philosophy.

Some states, one of which is California, have legislation *requiring* photographers to obtain a permit before using a minor as a model. These laws, known as Jackie Coogan legislation, impose complicated and expensive requirements on photographers who photograph minors. Therefore, it is advisable to check with a local attorney before you use a child model.

Since the legal concepts discussed in this chapter are still evolving, and since their treatment varies from state to state, you as a photographer would be well advised to work closely with a lawyer when a question arises regarding invasion of a right to privacy.

The following releases follow the principles that we have discussed. They are taken from *Business and Legal Forms for Photographers* by Tad Crawford. The forms can, of course, be modified to meet special needs that you may have.

Pocket Model Release

In consideration of _____ Dollars ($_____), receipt of which is acknowledged, I, _____ (print Model's name), do hereby give _____ (the Photographer), his or her assigns, licensees, successors in interest, legal representatives, and heirs the irrevocable right to use my name (or any fictional name), picture, portrait, or photograph in all forms and media and in all manners, including composite or distorted representations, for advertising, trade, or any other lawful purposes, and I waive any right to inspect or approve the finished version(s), including written copy that may be created and appear in connection therewith. I am of full age.* I have read this release and am fully familiar with its contents.

Witness_____   Signed_____
                                                                                    Model

Address_____   Address_____

Date _____, 19 ___

——————————————————— **Consent (if applicable)** ———————————————————

I am the parent or guardian of the minor named above and have the legal authority to execute the above release. I approve the foregoing and waive any rights in the premises.

Witness_____   Signed_____
                                                                           Parent or Guardian

Address_____   Address_____

Date _____, 19 ___

* Delete this sentence if the subject is a minor. The parent or guardian must then sign the consent.

Model Release

In consideration of _____ Dollars ($_____), and other valuable consideration, receipt of which is acknowledged, I, _____(print Model's name) do hereby give _____(the Photographer), his or her assigns, licensees, successors in interest, legal representatives, and heirs the irrevocable right to use my name (or any fictional name), picture, portrait, or photograph in all forms and in all media and in all manners, without any restriction as to changes or alterations (including but not limited to composite or distorted representations or derivative works made in any medium) for advertising, trade, promotion, exhibition, or any other lawful purposes, and I waive any right to inspect or approve the photograph(s) or finished version(s) incorporating the photograph(s), including written copy that may be created and appear in connection therewith. I hereby release and agree to hold harmless the Photographer, his or her assigns, licensees, successors in interest, legal representatives and heirs from any liability by virtue of any blurring, distortion, alteration, optical illusion, or use in composite form whether intentional or otherwise, that may occur or be produced in the taking of the photographs, or in any processing tending toward the completion of the finished product, unless it can be shown that they and the publication thereof were maliciously caused, produced, and published solely for the purpose of subjecting me to conspicuous ridicule, scandal, reproach, scorn, and indignity. I agree that the Photographer owns the copyright in these photographs and I hereby waive any claims I may have based on any usage of the photographs or works derived therefrom, including but not limited to claims for either invasion of privacy or libel. I am of full age* and competent to sign this release. I agree that this release shall be binding on me, my legal representatives, heirs, and assigns. I have read this release and am fully familiar with its contents.

Witness: _____   Signed: _____
                                                                    Model

Address: _____   Address: _____

                                           Date: _____, 19 _____

—————————————————————— Consent (if applicable) ——————————————————————

I am the parent or guardian of the minor named above and have the legal authority to execute the above release. I approve the foregoing and waive any rights in the premises.

Witness: _____   Signed: _____
                                                             Parent or Guardian

Address: _____   Address: _____

                                           Date: _____, 19 _____

* Delete this sentence if the subject is a minor. The parent or guardian must then sign the consent.

Property Release

In consideration of the sum of _____Dollars ($_____) and other valuable considera-

tion, receipt of which is hereby acknowledged, I, _____,

residing at _____, do, irrevoca-

bly authorize _____(the Photographer), his or her

assigns, licensees, successors in interest, legal representatives, and heirs to copyright, publish, and use in all forms and media and in all manners for advertising, trade, promotion, exhibition, or any other lawful purpose, images of the following property:

_____

_____

_____

which I own and have full and sole authority to license for such uses, regardless of whether said use is composite or distorted in character or form, whether said use is made in conjunction with my own name or with a fictitious name, or whether said use is made in color, black or white, or otherwise, or other derivative works are made through any medium.

I waive any right that I may have to inspect or approve the photograph(s) or finished version(s) incorporating the photographs, including written copy that may be used in connection therewith.

I am of full age and have every right to contract in my own name with respect to the foregoing matters. I agree that this release shall be binding on me, my legal representatives, heirs, and assigns. I have read the above authorization and release prior to its execution and I am fully cognizant of its contents.

Witness_____   Signed_____

Address_____   Address_____

Date _____, 19____

70

CENSORSHIP
AND OBSCENITY

The First Amendment of the United States Constitution states in part, "Congress shall make no law ... abridging the freedom of speech, or of the press." First Amendment absolutists insist that the words are all-encompassing and that no law should ever be enacted that places any restriction whatsoever on the free exercise of speech or press. Although a strict reading of the Constitution may support this opinion, the judiciary has never fully upheld it and has ruled that certain types of speech are not protected by the First Amendment.

Two theories have been used to justify exceptions to First Amendment protection. The first theory maintains that although certain expressions do normally deserve First Amendment protection, such protection will not be forthcoming if another right, either public or private, outweighs the citizen's First Amendment rights. Examples of speech (which has been defined as including photographs) that are not absolutely protected include defamatory remarks, remarks that advocate unlawful conduct, and remarks that invade someone's privacy. The second theory suggests that certain expressions do not constitute speech for purposes of First Amendment protection because they are without serious social value. Under this theory, courts often maintain that obscene works are not protected.

Prior Restraint

When the First Amendment was being written, the memory of the English licensing system, under which nothing could be published without prior approval, was still vivid in the minds of the framers of the Constitution. Some historians suggest that the First Amendment was written specifically to prevent such prior restraints. Today the First Amendment means more than freedom from prepublication censorship, but because of its potential for abuse, censorship before publication is still considered more serious than restrictions imposed after publication. The Supreme Court in *Near* v. *Minnesota* recognized that "liberty of the press ... has meant, principally although not exclusively, immunity from previous restraints and censorship."

Prior restraints impose an extreme burden upon the exercise of free speech since they limit open debate and the unfettered dissemination of knowledge. It is not surprising that the Supreme Court has almost universally found that it is unconstitutional to restrain speech prior to a determination of whether the speech is protected by the First Amendment.

Prohibition of Political Speech

A prior-restraint lawsuit generally begins with a request, often by the government, for a court order prohibiting publication of information already in the media's possession. Where controversial political speech is involved, the government may argue that publication will cause substantial and irreparable harm to the United States. In *New York Times Co.* v. *United States*, for example, the government tried to stop the publication of the Pentagon Papers, which detailed U.S. involvement in Vietnam prior to 1968. The government claimed that publication would prolong the war and embarrass the United States in the conduct of its diplomacy.

The Supreme Court found that the government's claim of potential injury to the U.S. was insufficient to justify prior restraint. The justices, although believing that publication would probably be harmful, were not persuaded that publication would "surely" cause the harm alleged.

Justice Potter Stewart agreed and wrote a concurring opinion emphasizing that the government must show that disclosure "will surely result in direct, immediate, and irreparable damage to our nation or its people."

In a later case, *United States* v. *The Progressive, Inc.*, the government used a similar argument: national security. In the *Progressive* case, the government sought to prohibit publication of a magazine article which detailed a method for constructing a hydrogen bomb. The government's case was weak for a variety of reasons, not the least of which was the fact that the alleged secrets were not then classified and had in fact been published in books, journals, magazines, and the government's own reports. Any diligent reporter could have uncovered the same information. Perhaps realizing the impossibility of meeting the test of "direct, immediate, irreversible harm" laid out in the 1971 Pentagon Papers case, the government abandoned the suit, but not until after raising the chilling threat of prior restraint.

Prohibition of Pretrial Publicity

Another kind of suppression of the free flow of information involves the restriction of pretrial publicity. Here the conflict is between the individual's right to a fair trial and the right of the press to its First Amendment guarantee of free speech. This conflict was addressed in *Nebraska Press Association* v. *Stuart*.

The Nebraska Press Association appealed a court order prohibiting the press from reporting on confessions and other information implicating an accused murderer after the murder of six family members had gained widespread public attention. The trial judge originally issued the order because he felt that pretrial publicity would make it difficult to select a jury that had not been exposed to prejudicial press coverage.

The Supreme Court nonetheless struck down the trial judge's order, finding that the impact of publicity on jurors was "speculative, dealing with factors unknown and unknowable." The justices went on to suggest alternatives to restraining all publication, including changing the location of the trial, postponing the trial, asking in-depth questions of prospective jury members during the selection process to determine bias, explicitly instructing the jury to consider only evidence presented at trial, and isolating the jury.

This decision appears to go far in requiring that other methods of pretrial precautions be taken, and that an order restricting press coverage be used only as a last resort. While this case involved press coverage, the same rule should apply to a photographer who wishes to publish a photograph of the scene of a crime or one which may be involved in litigation.

Prohibition of Commercial Speech

In other areas, however, the Court has been more tolerant of prior restraints. For example, the Court held in *Virginia State Board of Pharmacy* v. *Virginia Consumer Council* that prior restraints are sometimes permissible when purely commercial speech such as advertisements or other promotional material is involved. In that case the Court considered the constitutionality of a Virginia statute which prohibited pharmacists from advertising prices of prescription drugs. The Court held that the statute was unconstitutional and thereby rejected the notion that commercial speech is never entitled to First Amendment protection. However, the Court distinguished commercial speech from ordinary speech in discussing the application of the First Amendment to it. The Court reasoned that since commercial statements are generally objective in content, whether they are true or false can be readily determined. Thus, the Court believed that there was little or no threat of prior restraints being arbitrarily imposed. In addition, the Court maintained that commercial speech lacks the urgency which often accompanies noncommercial speech, so that any delay caused by the restraint while its justification is being argued would be relatively harmless. Since many of the dangers associated with prior restraints (such as suppression of political dissent) were not deemed to be present, the Court ruled that prior restraints of commercial speech are not always unconstitutional. Here, too, the rule announced by the court should apply to prior restraint imposed on photographs.

Prohibition of Obscene Speech

Prior restraints have also been upheld where the suppressed material was obscene, but the Supreme Court has imposed several procedural safeguards for this type of case. For example: (1) the accused must be given a prompt hearing; (2) the government agency making the accusation carries the burden of showing that the material is, in fact, obscene; (3) a valid final restraint can be issued only after a judicial proceeding; and (4) once the government agency has itself made a finding of obscenity, it must take action on its own behalf in a court of law to confirm its own finding.

Prior restraints on commercial speech and alleged obscenity are less often condemned by the courts because the immediately topical nature of and public interest in the free flow of "political speech" are not characteristic of commercial or sexual expressions; therefore, the public interest is not compromised as much by delays in publication of sexual expressions. As Justice John Harlan commented in *A Quantity of Cop-*

ies of Books v. *Kansas*, "sex is of constant but rarely particularly topical interest."

The Scope of Permissible Prior Restraints

It should be emphasized that the major presumption the Court made in *Near* v. *Minnesota* is still applicable; the chief purpose of the First Amendment's freedom of the press provision was to prevent prior restraints on publication. In *Near*, the Court listed only three situations which "might" justify prior restraint: (1) the need to prevent obstruction of a government's recruiting service, or to prevent publication of the sailing dates of transport ships or the number and location of troops; (2) failure to meet the requirements of decency, as in an obscene publication; and (3) the necessity of avoiding incitement to acts of violence and the overthrow by force of orderly government. These three exceptions, along with the requirements that the government prove with certainty that particular speech is unprotected and is likely to cause irreparable harm, limit the scope of permissible prior restraint.

It is worth noting that the Supreme Court has held that a school could suspend a student because of a speech he made containing numerous sexual metaphors, despite the student's claim of First Amendment protection. The Court felt that the school's right to maintain an appropriate educational environment for children outweighed the student's right of free speech.

Obscenity

Obscenity is perhaps the area where most of the censorship in this country has occurred.

A variety of laws are involved in regulating "obscene materials." Some state laws prohibit publication, distribution, public display or sales to minors of obscene material. Some city ordinances prohibit any commercial dealings in pornography whatsoever. Transporting obscene material across a state line or national border is forbidden by federal law, and it is a crime punishable by up to five years in jail to send obscene materials through the U.S. mail.

Since the private possession of obscene material is not unlawful, one who simply photographs material which could be categorized as obscene has not thereby violated obscenity laws. Of course, if the photographer himself publishes or distributes the material, liability can result. Otherwise, it is the magazine or book publisher who is at risk of violating the law. However, a photographer whose works involve especially graphic sexual scenes may be prevented from publishing or distributing those works because a court has previously declared the work to be obscene. In addition, the photographer whose work is declared obscene may face a lawsuit from his or her publisher, since many photographer-publisher contracts contain a warranty or indemnity clause stating that nothing in the work is obscene. In the event that the photograph is declared obscene, such a clause entitles the publisher to either sue the photographer directly for breach of warranty, or bill the photographer for any losses the publisher might have incurred in an obscenity suit.

Defining Obscenity

It has been the task of the Supreme Court, as the ultimate interpreter of the Constitution, to devise a definition of obscenity that is specific and at the same time flexible. It must be specific if it is to provide useful guidance to photographers and publishers, and it must be flexible to accommodate changes in social mores and ethics.

As the Court has attempted to formulate a definition which accomplishes these two objectives, the law of obscenity has undergone rapid changes.

The *Roth* Definition

In *Roth* v. *United States* a New York publisher and distributor of books, photographs, and magazines was convicted in the 1950s of violating a federal obscenity statute by mailing obscene circulars and advertising an obscene book. He appealed to the U.S. Supreme Court, claiming that his conduct was protected by the First Amendment. The Court rejected this argument and affirmed the conviction, but in the course of its opinion it did away with the standard which had been applied to obscenity cases since 1868, the ancient test devised by a British court in *Regina* v. *Hicklin*.

The *Regina* court had held that a publication which condemned certain practices of Roman Catholic priests in the confessional was obscene. There, the test for obscenity was "whether the tendency of the matter charged as obscenity is to deprave and corrupt those whose minds are open to such immoral influences and into whose hands a publication of this sort may fall." Because this test dictated that the material be judged according to the effect of an isolated excerpt upon persons of delicate sensibilities, it subjected to threat of censorship any adult treatment of sex, among other things, and endangered the right to publish and distribute many highly acclaimed literary works. In recognition of these problems the Court, in considering *Roth*, set forth a new standard: A work would be considered obscene if "to the average person, applying contemporary community standards, the dominant theme of the material taken as a whole appeals to prurient interest."

It was hoped that *Roth* would stabilize the law of obscenity, but confusion remained nonetheless. In *Jacobellis* v. *Ohio*, the Supreme Court reversed a conviction for violation of an Ohio statute which prohibited the possession and exhibition of obscene films. The Supreme Court held that the lower court had erroneously construed the phrase "contemporary community standards" to mean local rather than national standards. The Court thought that allowing local standards to govern would have the effect of denying some areas of the country access to materials that were acceptable in those areas, simply because publishers and distributors would be reluctant to risk prosecution under the laws of more conservative states where the same materials would be unacceptable. By applying a national standard to the case, the Court maintained that the film was not obscene. The question remains, however, of how to define the national standard. In *Roth*, it seems to have been found in the personal tastes and predilections of the majority of the justices, particularly in light of Justice Stewart's statement on the nature of obscenity: "I know it when I see it."

The *Memoirs* Definition

When the attorney general of Massachusetts requested a court order declaring the book *Fanny Hill* obscene, the Massachusetts courts ruled in his favor. On appeal, the Supreme Court in *Memoirs* v. *Massachusetts* reversed the Massachusetts courts, holding that the mere risk that a work *might* be exploited by advertisers because of its treatment of sexual matters is not sufficient to make it obscene. Instead, the Court held in a plurality opinion that the prosecution must establish three separate elements to prove obscenity:

> (a) the dominant theme of the material taken as a whole appeals to a prurient interest in sex; (b) the material is patently offensive because it affronts contemporary community standards relating to the description or representation of sexual matters; and (c) the material is utterly without redeeming social value.

However, even this three-part test has not brought clarity to the law of obscenity. In 1972, six years after the *Memoirs* decision, the Supreme Court was again confronted with a state court's overly broad definition of obscenity. The case was *Kois* v. *Wisconsin*.

In *Kois*, the Wisconsin state court convicted the publisher of an underground newspaper of two counts of violating a state obscenity statute which prohibited the dissemination of "lewd, obscene, or indecent written matter, pictures, sound recording, or film." The first count was for publication of an article that reported the arrest of one of the newspaper's photographers on a charge of possession of obscene material. Two relatively small pictures, showing a nude couple embracing in a sitting position, accompanied the article. The second count was for distributing a newspaper containing a poem entitled "Sex Poem," which was a frank, play-by-play account of the author's recollection of sexual intercourse.

The Supreme Court reversed the obscenity conviction, finding that, for the first count, the pictures were rationally related to an article that was clearly entitled to First Amendment protection. As for the second count, the poem had "some of the earmarks of an attempt at serious art."

The *Miller* Definition

The Supreme Court tried again to provide a workable definition in its 1973 *Miller* v. *California* decision. In this case, Marvin Miller sent five unsolicited brochures to a restaurant. The brochures advertised four books: *Intercourse, Man-Woman, Sex Orgies Illustrated*, and *An Illustrated History of Pornography*. Also included was a film entitled *Marital Intercourse*. The brochures contained pictures of men and women in a variety of sexual positions, with their genitals displayed.

In reviewing *Roth* and *Memoirs*, the Court concluded that one thing had been categorically settled: "Obscene material is unprotected by the First Amendment." But because any limitation on an absolute freedom of expression could lead to undesirable and dangerous censorship, it was deemed essential that state obscenity laws be limited in scope and properly applied. These concerns are manifest in the *Miller* obscenity test, which substantially modified the *Roth-Memoirs* test. The *Miller* test is:

> (a) whether "the average person, applying contemporary community standards" would find that the work, taken as a whole, appeals to the prurient interest, (b) whether the work depicts or describes in a patently offensive way, sexual conduct specifically defined by the applicable state law, and (c) whether the work, taken as a whole, lacks serious literary, artistic, political, or scientific values.

Thus, the *Roth-Memoirs* requirement that prosecutors prove that the challenged material is "utterly without social value" was replaced by a new standard which merely required the absence of "serious social value." Moreover, the Court upheld the right of a state to apply a local, rather than a national, standard in enforcing its obscenity laws.

The intent of *Miller* was to provide much clearer guidelines for protected speech, both to state legislatures enacting statutes and to prosecutors enforcing that legislation. *Miller* required that state statutes be more specific, so the states attempted to define the *Miller* test for their own communities. However, instead of clarifying the law, the hodge-podge of legislation spurred by *Miller* has only contributed to the vagueness, increased breadth, and chilling effect of obscenity legislation. Inconsistencies in the laws require the photographer to be aware of local statutes and ordinances in each area where distribution of a given photograph is planned.

Defining "Community Standards"

One of the greatest difficulties courts have had in applying the Miller test has involved defining "community" for the purposes of ascertaining moral standards. The Supreme Court said in 1974 that *Miller*'s effect "is to permit the juror in an obscenity case to draw on his own knowledge of the community from which he comes in deciding what conclusion an 'average person' would reach in a given case." The Court, however, does not require that the juror be instructed as to how large the relevant community is geographically. Instructions which direct the jury to apply "community standards" without specifying the boundaries of that community are acceptable. In reaffirming the idea that jurors are to draw on their own knowledge, the Court has emphasized that community standards are not to be defined legislatively.

Defining "Patently Offensive"

The Supreme Court in *Miller* provided some guidance as to the meaning of "patently offensive," indicating that the phrase refers to "hard-core" materials which, among other things, include "patently offensive representations or descriptions of ultimate sexual acts, normal or perverted, actual or simulated," and "patently offensive representations or descriptions of masturbation, excretory functions, and lewd exhibitions of the genitals." These examples indicate that materials less than "patently offensive" may well be entitled to First Amendment protection, and thus serve as a limitation on the states' power to arbitrarily define obscenity.

In *Jenkins* v. *Georgia*, the Supreme Court applied this standard to the Academy Award-winning film *Carnal Knowledge*. A Georgia court had convicted the defendant after a jury determined that the film was obscene. Although the Court recognized that the issue of obscenity was primarily a question of fact to be determined by the jury, it was not willing to grant the jury unlimited license in making that determination. Because the Court decided that the film was not sufficiently hardcore to be considered patently offensive, it reversed the jury's decision and the resulting conviction.

Defining the "Prurient Interest" of the "Average Person"

According to the ruling in *Miller*, to be judged obscene, a work must appeal to the "prurient interest" of the "average person." *Prurient interest* is an elusive concept, but that did not stop the Supreme Court from attempting to define it in *Roth* as that which "beckons to a shameful, morbid, degrading, unhealthy, or unwholesome interest in sex." Some states have attempted to write their own definition of prurient interest into their obscenity statutes. One such attempt that was challenged as overly broad led to yet another Supreme Court decision on obscenity in *Brockett* v. *Spokane Arcades, Inc.*

The statute challenged in *Brockett* defined obscene matter as that appealing to the prurient interest, which was further defined as "that which incites lasciviousness or lust." The Supreme Court held that by including lust in its definition of prurient, the statute extended to material which merely stimulated normal sexual responses. Thus, the statute was overly broad and unconstitutional. The Court indicated that material said to appeal to prurient interests is to be judged by its impact on the normal person, not by its effect on those who are easily influenced or unusually sensitive. Thus, a jury is not to consider the effect the material in question would have on children or adolescents under eighteen. These statements by the Court raise the possibility of a defense argument that if a work obviously appeals to a bizarre or deviant sexual appetite, acquittal is required because the "average person" is not affected. A widely recognized exception to the "average person" standard has been established by the Court, however, where it can be shown that a given book, magazine, or film was designed for and distributed to a well-defined deviant group.

The issue of whether material appeals primarily to the prurient interest may be influenced by the manner in which it is advertised. Evidence of an advertising practice known legally as "pandering" may contribute to the likelihood that a work will be declared obscene. Pandering occurs when materials are marketed by emphasizing their sexually provocative nature.

The relevance of pandering was first determined by the Supreme Court in 1966, in *Ginzburg* v. *U.S.* In *Ginzburg*, the Supreme Court reviewed a conviction under a federal obscenity statute for distribution of several publications containing erotic materials which, because they were of some value to psychiatrists and other professionals, were not in and of themselves obscene. However, since the defendants had portrayed the materials as salacious and lewd in their marketing, and had indiscriminately distributed those works to the general public, the trial court had found the materials to be obscene. The Supreme Court affirmed, stating that evidence of pandering is relevant to the question of obscenity.

The Supreme Court again upheld the relevance of pandering in *Hamling* v. *United States*. In that case, the Court made it clear that where the obscenity question is a close one, evidence of pandering may be considered. Such evidence is but one factor in determining whether a work is obscene, however, and does not replace the *Miller* test.

Thematic Obscenity

Thematic obscenity refers to obscenity that is more or less the central theme of a work, and thus is relevant to the ideas the work intends to express. Such material is not completely beyond the states' reach if it is in fact obscene. At the same time, the Supreme Court is extremely suspicious of state obscenity statutes that appear to prohibit sexually explicit materials which convey certain ideas, rather than sexually explicit (and patently offensive) materials in and of themselves.

The Supreme Court addressed thematic obscenity in *Kingsley International Pictures Corp.* v. *Regents of the University of New York*. In this case, the Court reviewed a New York statute which forbade licenses for the exhibition of motion pictures that portrayed "acts of sexual immorality ... as desirable, acceptable, or as a proper pattern of behavior." Application of the statute had resulted in denial of a license for *Lady Chatterley's Lover*, a film that portrayed an adulterous relationship.

The Court found that the New York statute went beyond regulating the depiction of patently offensive sexual acts and, in effect, prevented the expression of an idea—namely, that an adulterous relationship could under some circumstances be condoned. Since the right to express ideas is expressly protected by the First Amendment, and since the statute denied that right, the statute was deemed unconstitutional.

Another attempt to suppress thematic obscenity was overturned by the Court in 1962 in *Manual Enterprises* v. *Day*. This time the Court held that a magazine for homosexuals was not obscene. Obscenity, it said, requires proof of two elements: (1) patent offensiveness and (2) appeal to prurient interest. Since pictures in the magazine under attack were found to be no more objectionable than the pictures of female

81

nudes that society tolerates in other magazines, they could not be prohibited simply because they conveyed the idea of homosexuality.

Federal Statutes

Under the anti-pandering law, people who receive any pandering advertisements which those people find erotically arousing or sexually provocative can notify the Postal Service that they wish to receive no further mailings from the sender, following which the Postal Service is required to issue an order directing the sender of such advertisements to refrain from further mailings to those recipients. The U.S. Supreme Court upheld the validity of the anti-pandering law in *Rowan* v. *United States Post Office Dept*. In that case the Supreme Court said that a "mailer's right to communicate must stop at the mail box of an unreceptive addressee."

The Postal Reorganization Act of 1970 contains a provision that prohibits the mailing of sexually oriented advertisements to any person who has requested that his name be placed on the Postal Service list of persons desiring not to receive sexually oriented advertising. This law is popularly known as the Goldwater Amendment, and was enacted in an effort to prevent the flow of vulgar or pornographic material into the home of anyone not wishing to be subjected to such mail, while preserving the rights of those who want to receive such material through the mail. The notice authorized under the Goldwater Amendment affects all mailers and not just a particular mailer.

A year's subscription to a copy of the list of those who do not wish to receive sexually oriented ads can be obtained from the Postal Service by a deposit of $5,000 and subsequent payment of charges not to exceed $10,000, including the deposit. A sexually oriented advertisement is defined as:

> any advertisement that depicts, in actual or simulated form, or explicitly describes, in a predominantly sexual context, human genitalia, any act of natural or unnatural sexual intercourse, any act of sadism or masochism, or any other erotic subject directly related to the foregoing. [However] material otherwise within the definition of this subsection shall be deemed not to constitute a sexually oriented advertisement if it constitutes only a small and insignificant part of the whole of a single catalog, book, periodical or other work the remainder of which is not primarily devoted to sexual matters.

Child Pornography Legislation

Attempts to regulate pornography have also been made by legislators enacting child pornography laws. This legislation is designed to curb sexual abuse of children by making it unlawful to use children in explicit sexual performances or pornographic pictures. The Supreme Court has been relatively supportive of state efforts to outlaw pornography dealing with children. In the 1982 case of *New York* v. *Ferber*, the Court held that a state may ban the distribution of materials showing children engaged in sexual conduct even though the material is not legally obscene. State child-pornography laws vary widely. The photographer who plans to sell any pictures of children in sexual circumstances would be well advised to consult with a lawyer.

In April 1990, the U.S. Supreme Court upheld a child pornography statute in Ohio despite a strong dissent by Justice Brennan on the vagueness of the statute. A short time later, in Ohio, the Cincinnati Contemporary Arts Center and its Director faced criminal prosecution for possession of child pornography when the Center displayed Robert Mapplethorpe's homoerotic photographs, some of which were photographs of naked children. Both were later found not guilty.

Also in 1990, Federal Bureau of Investigation agents raided the studio of San Francisco photographer Jock Sturges. Sturges, who is known for his black-and-white portraits of families in the nude had asked his film processor to make negatives from color slides he had taken of some of the children he had photographed. The pictures had been taken with the permission of all the children's parents and the negatives were to be used to make color prints that Sturges intended to give as gifts to the families.

The police were notified by the San Francisco branch of Newell Colour, a photo processing laboratory based in London. Sturges' film processor had taken the negatives there to be printed. State law requires such commercial processing laboratories to report photographs that may violate child pornography statutes. Failing to do so may subject them to loss of business licenses. Sturges' film processor was arrested which led to the raid of Sturges' studio, and confiscation of much of his work. Duke Diedrich, a spokesman for the Bureau said it was the Bureau's policy to investigate when it seemed "the focus of the photos is directed toward the genitalia."

In 1988, Congress passed the Child Protection and Obscenity Act. This law prohibits the use of computers to advertise, distribute, or receive child pornography and the sale, or possession with intent to sell, of child pornography on federal lands. Producers of sexually explicit materials are required to keep records of the age and identity of each performer participating in sexually explicit conduct.

Forfeiture or Closure Legislation

Photographers should be aware that some states have statutes that make it a crime or a public nuisance to disseminate or exhibit obscene material. Usually, these statutes allow the authorities to close or even cause the owner to forfeit the use of the property from which the obscene materials were disseminated. Under some of these statutes authorities may enforce closure or forfeiture of premises even though the material disseminated was "lewd" or "indecent" rather than actually obscene. Some courts have found these statutes to be unconstitutional prior restraints of nonobscene material. However, other courts have upheld forfeiture statutes, reasoning that no closure or forfeiture takes place until there has been a judicial determination of whether the disseminated material was actually obscene.

Informal Censorship

There is the possibility that government funding could be distributed in such a way as to constitute informal censorship. The problem is illustrated by the case of *Advocates for the Arts* v. *Thompson*. In that case the plaintiff, Granite Publications, was to receive a grant from the New Hampshire Commission on the Arts, which was funded largely by the National Endowment for the Arts. The commission withdrew its pledge of funding upon discovering that a poem previously published by Granite was, in the commission's opinion, obscene. Granite sued, alleging that its First Amendment rights had been violated. The federal court ruled in favor of the arts commission.

Although the Court was not willing to rule that the poem was obscene under the *Miller* test, neither was it willing to intrude upon the discretion of the arts commission to determine which projects would or would not receive government funds. As long as it could be argued that the commission's selections were based on the issue of artistic or literary merit, the First Amendment was not violated. The Court did intimate that the commission might not have exercised the best judgment with respect to the poem. Nevertheless, the Court refused to place itself in a position of being the final arbiter of questions of literary merit. Moreover, the Court refused to require the commission to draw up narrow standards and guidelines by which artistic merit could be judged, since these qualities are by their very nature subjective.

The Court concluded that refusal of the government to provide funds for the arts will not normally constitute censorship, since such refusal does not prohibit the publication of a given work, although inability to publish may be the practical result. Photographers may therefore find that their work is unacceptable to publishers who are concerned about this informal type of censorship. This is not to say that government funding agencies are completely immune from attack on the basis of constitutional rights. The court in Thompson did suggest that, should an agency develop a "pattern of discrimination impinging upon the basic First Amendment rights to free and full debate on matters of public interest," an argument concerning the photographer's constitutional rights might have merit.

Once a work has received some form of government funding, the withdrawal of the government sponsorship may be a First Amendment violation. Thus in *American Council for the Blind* v. *The Librarian of Congress* it was held that Congress's refusal to continue funding for the purpose of putting into Braille and recording *Playboy* magazine infringed the constitutional rights of the plaintiff, the American Council for the Blind.

"Censorship" by Film Processors

Courts have upheld the right of a film processor to refuse to process or return film which the processor deemed obscene. Processors have been allowed to retain allegedly obscene film on three theories: first, that return of the film might make the processor liable under a state obscenity statute; second, that the owner has no right to film which constitutes obscene contraband; and, third, existence of an implied or express contract term that the developer is not required to process or return films of obscene subject matter. In *Penthouse Enter., Ltd.* v. *Eastman Kodak Co.*, the court held that a film processor had the right to decide what it would refuse to process so long as its policies were applied uniformly, and no First Amendment rights were violated since no state action was involved and the film processor did not censor or restrict what the magazine could publish.

Predicting Liability

As I have indicated here, whether or not a photograph is likely to be deemed obscene under the *Miller* test is extremely difficult to predict. Courts have experienced numerous problems in applying the *Miller* test, and there is no indication that these problems are likely to be resolved in the near future.

Perhaps the most significant barrier to predictability in obscenity cases is that obscenity is a factual question to be determined by a jury. Presumably, juries are composed of reasonable persons, but it has long been recognized that reasonable persons may disagree. Consequently it is not particularly surprising that different juries have come up with different results in obscenity cases involving essentially the same facts and issues.

Censorship in the United States is far from a fading issue or a shrinking problem for the photographer. In fact, passage and enforcement of even more restrictive obscenity laws may be on the horizon. This scenario is recommended to the American people in the report of the United States Attorney General's Commission on Pornography released July 9, 1986.

The eleven-member "Meese Commission," appointed in May of 1985 and stacked unabashedly with anti-vice prosecutors and activists, reviewed social research and conducted over 300 hours of emotional hearings which one critic has referred to as a "show trial in which pornography was found guilty."

The commission wrestled unsuccessfully with the problem of defining pornography, and in the end was unable to articulate any category of sexual imagery which it would consider harmless, ultimately overturning the findings of the 1970 report of the President's Commission on Pornography which had concluded there was no evidence that sexually explicit material caused antisocial behavior.

The Meese Commission not only recommended passage of new state obscenity laws, but also endorsed citizen action groups and provided instructions for canvassing local bookstores and for organizing demonstrations, boycotts, and other grass-roots censorship-oriented activities.

How, then, is the photographer to predict whether a particular jury might reasonably find a photograph to be obscene? You probably cannot make this prediction, at least not without the assistance of a lawyer familiar with the relevant decisions. By analyzing the various obscenity cases in which the defendant was convicted and contrasting them with those in which the defendant was acquitted, and by staying on top of any new obscenity laws which may be enacted in the future, an attorney should be able to provide a fairly accurate prediction as to whether the work in question will or will not be considered obscene. Unfortunately, graphic material such as pictures and films is much more often found to be obscene than written material.

Other Censorship Problems

Censorship of obscene material is only one limitation the government places on photographers' First Amendment rights. In addition, the government forbids the photographing of money or postage stamps, unless certain requirements are met, as well as the photographing of U.S. military installations that contain secret equipment or facilities. Reproductions of postage stamps or money must be less than three-fourths or more than one and one-half times the size of the original. In addition, reproductions of money must be in black and white.

Also, the federal government and most of the states have enacted flag-desecration statutes that impose civil or criminal liability on persons who deface or mutilate a flag. These statutes were enacted in response to the flag burnings by protestors against the Vietnam War and against civil rights abuses. Generally, flag-desecration statutes are designed to prevent breaches of the peace which might result from improper use of and disrespect to the flag. Thus, *People* v. *Von Rosen* held that magazine publication of photographs of a nude girl covered by an American flag, though disrespectful, did not violate a state flag-desecration statute because the photographs were not likely to bring about a breach of the peace. However, some courts have recognized other purposes to be served by flag-desecration statutes. In *People* v. *Keough*, the court found that publication of photographs of a female clothed only in an American flag and a pair of boots, posing with a soldier, was sufficient to be a violation of a state flag-desecration statute because the photographs cast contempt upon the American flag.

Many flag-desecration statutes require that the disrespectful display of the flag be a public one. Under these statutes, a photographer could not be liable for any disrespectful flag photograph until it was published.

In the District of Columbia, it is an offense to use the United States flag or any representation thereof for advertising or commercial purposes. Some courts have found that commercial use of flags violates flag-desecration statutes even though those statutes contain no specific provisions against commercial use.

Courtroom Proceedings

In 1937, the American Bar Association adopted Canon 35 of the Canons of Judicial Ethics prohibiting broadcast and photographic coverage of court proceedings. As far as the federal courts are concerned, Rule 53 of the Federal Rules of Criminal Procedure prohibits "taking of photographs in the courtroom during the progress of judicial proceedings." This rule is still in effect today, but applies only to criminal trials in federal courts.

Generally speaking, the propriety of granting or denying permission to the media to broadcast, record, or photograph court proceedings involves weighing the constitutional guarantees of freedom of the press and the right to a public trial on the one hand, and, on the other hand, the due process rights of the defendant and the power of the courts to control their proceedings in order to permit the fair and impartial administration of justice.

There appears to be general agreement that, based on the right of freedom of the press, representatives of the media have a constitutional right to broadcast, record, or photograph court proceedings. However, in cases in which media representatives have claimed that court rules and orders prohibiting broadcast or photographic coverage of judicial proceedings infringed upon the freedom of the press, the prohibitions have been upheld as reasonable and proper attempts to preserve courtroom decorum and to protect the rights of defendants. The courts have also rejected claims by press representatives that such prohibitions deprived them of rights protected by federal civil rights laws.

There also appears to be general agreement that the constitutional right to a public trial does not give the press the right to broadcast, record, or photograph court proceedings, since the right to a public trial is for the benefit of the defendant, and since the requirement of a public trial is satisfied when members of the press and public are permitted to attend a trial and to report what transpires. In a number of cases, the courts have held that court orders prohibiting broadcast or photographic coverage of criminal trials were proper attempts to protect the rights of defendants, and that the orders therefore did not deny the defendants their right to a public trial.

The Supreme Court ruled in *Chandler* v. *Florida* that the due process rights of an accused are not inherently denied by television coverage, and that no constitutional rule specifically prohibits the states from permitting broadcast or photographic coverage of criminal trial proceedings. The Court pointed out, however, that, depending upon the circumstances under which such coverage takes place, a due process violation might result.

A number of states have permitted such coverage on either a permanent or experimental basis. Therefore, the photographer is advised to consult the applicable rules in order to determine the specific types of equipment which may be permitted, the location of the equipment in the courtroom, and the number of media representatives who may be permitted access to the courtroom to operate such equipment.

Court rules frequently prescribe the specific conditions under which representatives of the media may use broadcasting, recording, or photographic to record judicial proceedings. The courts generally have reasoned that a complete prohibition against broadcast or photographic coverage is not required in order to protect the rights of trial participants or the dignity of court proceedings, and that such coverage does in fact serve the public interest.

GOVERNMENTAL
LICENSES AND
RESTRICTIONS

The purpose of state and local licensing statutes is threefold: to generate revenue; to regulate entry into certain trades and professions; and to regulate the standards to which those in a particular trade or profession are held. The types of professions that states generally regulate are those that could potentially present a threat to the general public. These professions usually include health care professionals, building contractors, and the like.

Whether or not it is appropriate for a state to require a photographer to be licensed has been a matter of some controversy. Generally, such licensing statutes have been held unconstitutional as interfering with an individual's First Amendment rights. As photography poses no threat to the general public, it has been concluded that a state does not have the authority to regulate the profession.

There was one brief period in 1938 when the licensing of photographers was held to be constitutional by the North Carolina Supreme Court. That same court later, in 1949, reversed its position and struck down the licensing scheme. Subsequently, there have been a number of other state supreme courts who have similarly ruled licensing requirements for photographers as unconstitutional.

In 1970, the South Dakota Supreme Court held unconstitutional a city ordinance requiring all itinerant or transient photographers to be licensed and bonded. In this case, the court concluded the ordinance was invalid because there was no similarly imposed burden on local photographers. Thus, the ordinance was overburdening to non-local photographers involved in interstate commerce.

The Photographer's Right of Access and Restrictions

As important as the photographic subject's right to privacy is the photographer's right to take pictures. Neither of these rights is absolute; rather, the subject's right of privacy and the photographer's right to take pictures are the mirror image of one another and one right ends where the other begins.

Generally, photographers have a right to take pictures so long as they do not invade their subjects' privacy or make a public nuisance of themselves. Ordinarily, you can take pictures in concert halls, theaters, museums, hospitals, and nursing homes so long as you do not infringe copyrights by doing so and so long as the institution in question has no clear rules or regulations to the contrary. If an institution has a clearly posted prohibition against taking photographs, you may be liable for trespass if you proceed to take pictures. In addition, there are some statutes which prohibit photographing certain buildings or sites such as the federal prohibition against photographing post offices or military institutions. The federal government also prohibits the commercial exploitation of photographs of federal land without express permission.

Photographs of Buildings, Sites, or Objects

Photographers should be aware that owners of buildings, locations, or objects may have a protected interest in exploiting images of those properties. The exclusive right to exploit the likenesses of one's buildings, land, or other possessions is technically a property right, rather than a right of privacy, but the legal repercussions of photographing a building may be equivalent to the legal consequences of photographing a person. In *New York World's Fair 1964–65 Corp.* v. *Colourpicture*

Pub. Inc., the court held that the defendant's photograph of a unique building had invaded a property right of the plaintiff when the photographer commercially exploited the photograph. For this reason, a photographer should obtain a property release from the owner of unique buildings, landmarks, automobiles, and other forms of property when they are to be photographed. When in doubt about the item to be photographed, prudence would dictate that you should err on the side of caution and obtain the release. A well-drafted document will grant you the right to photograph the item in question and commercially exploit it. See the sample release at the end of this chapter.

There are also certain restrictions in photographing governmental items. The U.S. presidential seal, for example, may not be reproduced in any form without the proper authorization. U.S. currency and stamps may be reproduced only in black and white, and only if the reproduction is at least 150% larger or 75% smaller than the currency's actual size.

It is a federal offense to "reproduce, manufacture or use" the characters "Smokey Bear" and "Woodsy Owl." Those characters were created by the United States Forest Service, which is a division of the Department of Agriculture.

In 1993, however, a federal district court held that the U.S. Forest Service was not justified in relying on this statute to prevent the use of a chain-saw wielding Smokey Bear by an environmental organization. The court stated that this depiction of Smokey Bear was purely expressive, noncommercial speech which is protected under the First Amendment. Further, the court stated that such a use was unlikely to cause confusion or to dilute the value of Smokey Bear to help prevent forest fires. Therefore, the statute was unconstitutionally applied to the satirical poster.

The photographing of prisons may also be restricted. In one case, the Governor of Florida initially upheld his director of prisons' position on the denial of an already issued permit to film an anti-capital-punishment movie in a state prison. After the matter apparently received some adverse publicity, he reversed his position and allowed the film to be made.

Photojournalists tend to have somewhat more legal protection of their right of access to subjects if those subjects are newsworthy. The United States Supreme Court has recognized that the First Amendment protects the media's right to publish news. However, news media have no constitutional right of access to the scenes of crime or disaster when the general public is excluded. Basically, the United States Supreme Court has held that as long as restrictions treat the media and the public equally, they are constitutional. However, some recent cases indicate that news professionals may have more rights than the general public. This is particularly true for photographers of courtroom proceedings. The vast majority of states permit such access, though the rules and restrictions vary from state to state.

At the time of this writing, Indiana, Missouri, Mississippi, and South Dakota are the only states that do not allow photographic coverage in the courtroom to at least some extent. Some states have permitted coverage on an experimental basis.

In almost all states, prior consent of the presiding judge is required, and the judge retains control over coverage throughout the proceedings.

In most states, coverage is prohibited in cases involving juveniles, sex-crime victims, domestic relations, and trade secrets. Coverage of jurors and certain witnesses is also restricted.

Guidelines provided by the court generally include provisions on media equipment, lights, number of media personnel, types of cameras, position of equipment operators, and movement in the courtroom. For more information about photographing courtroom proceedings, contact: Information Service, National Center for State Courts, 300 Newport Avenue, Williamsburg, VA 23187-8798 (804) 253-2000.

Newsworthy events often occur in public places such as streets, sidewalks, or parks. These places are public forums because they are open to the public and few restrictions are placed on the activities which may take place in them. Reporters can be barred from covering activities in public forums only if news-gathering restrictions are reasonable.

In New York City, there are several sections of the administrative code that require permits in order to take photographs, film motion pictures, or to telecast in public places. Other sections of New York City's code forbid the use of tripods in public parks. (For a sample City of New York application and permit for still photography, see the end of this chapter.)

Not all property owned by the government is considered a public forum. Federal Courthouses, jails, government offices, and city halls are not usually open for general, public use. Therefore, in many cases courts have not allowed the media access to such property.

When municipal property is not operated by the municipality, the media have only the same right of access as the general public.

Many newsworthy events occur on private property. Property owners may restrict access to their homes, businesses, shopping centers, and privately-owned housing developments. Even when property owners have not barred access, they have been able to obtain damages for trespass or invasion of privacy when they did not consent to the journalist's entry. A key issue in such cases is whether the owner's silence was the effective equivalent of consent. In a Florida case, an invasion-of-privacy suit was brought against a newspaper for publishing a photograph of the silhouette of the body of a seventeen-year-old girl killed in a house fire. The fire marshal and a police sergeant investigating the fire invited the news media into the burned-out home to cover the story. In court, they testified that their invitation was standard practice. The property owner, who was the victim's mother, was out of town at the time of the fire. Therefore, she was not present to be asked for permission. Clearly, the fire was of great public interest because of the damage done to the house, because a person had died, and because arson was suspected. The court found implied consent and ruled in favor of the media, with the qualification that if the owner had been present and objected to the reporter's presence, the reporter might have been liable for damages.

Photojournalists should be aware that state constitutions may provide greater protection for the media than does the United States Constitution. In California, the state constitution guarantees access to news on private business property.

However, if the police order you not to enter an area in pursuit of news, you are risking arrest, prosecution, and liability by disregarding the order, whether or not the property in question is public or privately owned. In *Stahl* v. *Oklahoma*, several reporters were arrested for following anti-nuclear-power demonstrators onto a privately-owned power plant site. The owner of the land, the Public Service Co. of Oklahoma, had denied both the public and the media access to the plant. The court treated the plant as a government entity because the power company's activities were heavily regulated by the state and federal government. Nonetheless, the judge fined the reporters for criminal trespass, ruling that the First Amendment does not guarantee access to property simply because it is owned or controlled by the government nor does the First Amendment protect reporters from arrest and prosecution if they have broken the law while gathering news.

In 1991, the Connecticut Appellate Court affirmed a newspaper photographer's conviction for interfering with a police officer's performance of duty. The photographer refused to move from the immediate vicinity of a fatal car accident, despite numerous police requests, insisting it was his constitutional right to remain.

Police departments across the country are under pressure to develop guidelines governing their relationship with the media. If a police department provides guidelines governing access to crime or accident scenes and issues press credentials, the guidelines must not result in the arbitrary denial of access to certain journalists. In *Sherrill* v. *Knight*, the court held that if an agency establishes a policy of admitting the media, even though the public is barred, media access cannot later be denied arbitrarily or for less than compelling reasons. It also ruled that agencies must publish the standards that will be used in deciding whether an applicant is eligible to receive a press pass and that journalists who are denied press passes must be provided with reasons for the denial and given an opportunity to appeal.

THE CITY OF NEW YORK
OFFICE OF THE MAYOR
OFFICE OF FILM, THEATRE AND BROADCASTING

1697 Broadway
New York, NY 10019
Telephone (212) 489-6710
FAX (212) 262-7677

PATRICIA REED SCOTT
COMMISSIONER

PERMIT FOR STILL PHOTOGRAPHY

This application is for permission to use the streets and sidewalks of the City of New York subject to the City's jurisdiction to take location photography and is to be filed with the Permit Division, 1697 Broadway, 6th Floor, New York, NY 10019 (212) 489-6710

REPRESENTATIVE_____DATE OF APPLICATION_____

COMPANY_____PHONE_____

ADDRESS_____

LOCATION(S) OF PHOTOGRAPHY_____

_____

_____

DATE(S) OF PHOTOGRAPHY_____TIME_____

CAMERA FORMAT/ OTHER EQUIPMENT_____

NUMBER IN GROUP_____VEHICLES_____

PROPS_____

DESCRIPTION OF PHOTOGRAPH/ SCENE_____

_____

The applicant agrees to indemnify the City of New York and to be solely and absolutely liable upon any and all claims, suits, and judgments against the City and/or the applicant, his (it's) employees or otherwise. The applicant further agrees to comply with all pertinent provision of New York laws, rules and regulations, including, but not limited to Sec. 20-453 of New York City Administrative Code which prohibits general vending on the streets of the City of New York without a license issued by the Department of Consumer Affairs.
This Permit does not include parking privileges.

_____
SIGNATURE OF APPLICANT

*OFFICE USE ONLY, DO NOT WRITE BELOW THIS LINE*_____

_____   _____
DATE   PERMIT COORDINATOR

94

6

ORGANIZING
AS A BUSINESS

One of the reasons—perhaps the primary reason—why photographers like their work is that they feel they have escaped the stultifying atmosphere of the dress-for-success business world. But they have not escaped it entirely. The same laws, although not the same culture, that govern the billion-dollar auto industry govern the photographer. This being the case, you might as well learn how you can use some of those laws to your advantage.

Any professional person knows that survival requires careful financial planning. Yet few photographers realize the importance of selecting the *form* for their business. Most photographers have little need for the sophisticated organizational structures utilized in industry, but since photographers must pay taxes, obtain loans, and expose themselves to potential liability every time they take photographs and sell their work, it only makes sense to structure the business so as to minimize these concerns.

Every business has an organizational form best suited to it. When I counsel photographers on organizing their businesses, I usually adopt a two-step approach. First, we discuss various aspects of taxes and liability in order to decide which of the basic forms is best. There are only a handful of basic forms: the *sole proprietorship*; the *partnership*; the *corporation*; a few hybrids; and the newest business form, the *limited liability company*. Once we have decided which of these is appropriate, we go into the organizational details such as partnership agreements or corporate papers. These documents define the day-to-day operations of a business, and therefore, must be tailored to individual situations.

What I offer here is an explanation of features of these various of business organizations, including their advantages and disadvantages. This should give you some idea of which form might be best for you.

I will discuss potential problems but, since I cannot go into a full discussion of the more intricate details, you should consult an attorney before deciding to adopt any particular structure. My purpose here is to facilitate your communication with your lawyer and to enable you to better understand the choices available.

The American Dream: Sole Proprietorship

The technical name "sole proprietorship" may be unfamiliar to you, but you may be operating under this form now. A sole proprietorship is an unincorporated business owned by one person. Although not peculiar to the United States, it was, and still is, the backbone of the American dream, to the extent that personal freedom follows economic freedom. As a form of business it is elegant in its simplicity. All it requires is a little money and work. Legal requirements are few and simple. In most localities, professionals such as photographers are not required to have a business license, but, if you wish to operate the business under a name other than your own, the name must be registered with the state and, in some cases, the county in which you are doing business. With this detail taken care of, you are in business.

Disadvantages of Sole Proprietorship

There are many financial risks involved in operating your business as a sole proprietor. If you recognize any of these dangers as a real threat, you probably should consider an alternative form of organization.

If you are the sole proprietor of a business venture, the property you personally own is at stake. In other words, if for any reason you owe more than the dollar value of your business, your creditors can force a sale of most of your personal property to satisfy the debt. Thus, if one of your photographs is defamatory, an invasion of someone's privacy, or an infringement of a copyright, you could find that you are financially responsible for paying judgment.

For many risks, insurance is available which will shift the loss from you to an insurance company, but there is no insurance against a sudden rise in the cost of supplies or raw materials such as film or darkroom chemicals. In any case, insurance policies do have monetary limits. Furthermore, insurance premiums can be quite high, and there is no way to accurately predict or plan for future increases in premiums. (For further discussion on insurance, see chapter 9 on leases and insurance.) These hazards, as well as many other uncertain economic factors, can drive a small business into bankruptcy, and that, in turn, could force you into personal bankruptcy; if you are the sole proprietor.

Taxes for the Sole Proprietor

The sole proprietor is taxed on all profits of the business and may deduct losses. Of course, the rate of taxation will change with increases in income. A particularly successful year can leave the sole proprietor no better off financially than in the less successful years, due to the higher tax bracket and increased expenses.

Fortunately, there are ways to ease the tax burden. For instance, you can establish an approved IRA or pension plan, deducting a specified amount of your net income for placement into the pension plan, or into an interest-bearing account, or into approved government securities or mutual funds to be withdrawn later when you are in a lower tax bracket. There are severe restrictions, however, for withdrawal of this money prior to retirement age.

For further information on these tax-planning devices, you should contact your local IRS office and ask for free pamphlets. Or you might wish to use the services of an accountant experienced in dealing with photographers' tax considerations.

Partnership

A partnership is defined by most state laws as an association of two or more persons to conduct, as co-owners, a business for profit. Two photographers can form a partnership. This arrangement can be very attractive to beginning photographers because it allows them to pool their money, equipment, and contacts.

When a photographer agrees to work with another on a project or when a photographer and writer get together and agree to produce a manuscript accompanied by photographs, this also constitutes a partnership. No formalities are required. In fact, in some cases people have been held to be partners even though they never had any intention of forming a partnership. For example, if you lend a friend some money to start a business and the friend agrees to pay you a certain percentage of whatever profit is made, you may be your friend's partner in the eyes of the law even though you take no part in running the business. This is important because each partner is subject to unlimited personal liability for the debts of the partnership. Also, each partner is liable for the negligence of another partner and for the partnership's employees when a negligent act occurs in the course of business. In effect, each partner is considered an employee of the partnership.

This means that if you are getting involved in a partnership, you should be careful in three areas. First, since the involvement of a partner increases your potential liability, you should choose a responsible partner. Second, the partnership should be adequately insured to protect both the assets of the partnership and the personal assets of each partner. Finally, it is a good idea for you to draw up a written agreement between you and your partner in order to avoid any misunderstandings or confusion in the future.

As I have already mentioned, no formalities are required to create a partnership. If the partners do not have a formal agreement defining the terms of the partnership—such as control of the partnership or the distribution of profits—state law will determine the terms. State laws are based on the fundamental characteristics of the typical partnership as it has existed through the ages. The most important of these legally-presumed characteristics are:

- No one can become a member of a partnership without the unanimous consent of all partners.
- All partners have an equal vote in the management of the partnership regardless of the size of their interest in it.
- All partners share equally in the profits and losses of the partnership no matter how much capital they have contributed.
- A simple majority vote is required for decisions in the ordinary course of business, and a unanimous vote is required to change the fundamental character of the business.
- A partnership is terminable at will by any partner; a partner can withdraw from the partnership at any time, and this withdrawal causes a dissolution of the partnership.

Most state laws contain a provision that allows the partners to make their own agreements regarding the management structure and division of profits that best suits the needs of the individual partners.

Taxes

A partnership does not possess any tax advantages over a sole proprietorship. Each partner pays tax on his or her share of the profits, whether distributed or retained, and each is entitled to the same proportion of the partnership deductions and credits. The partnership must prepare for the IRS an annual information return known as Schedule K-1, Form 1065, which details each partner's share of income, credits, and deductions, and against which the IRS can check the individual returns filed by the partners.

The Limited Partnership

The limited partnership is a hybrid containing elements of both the partnership and the corporation. A limited partnership may be formed by parties who wish to invest in a store and, in return, to share in its profits, but who seek to limit their risk to the amount of their investment. The law provides for such limited risk, but only so long as the limited partner plays no active role in the day-to-day management and operation of the business. In effect, the limited partner is very much like an investor who buys a few shares of stock in a corporation but has no significant role in running the corporation. In order to establish a limited partnership, it is necessary to have one or more general partners who run the business and who have full personal liability, and one or more limited partners who play a passive role.

To form a limited partnership, a document must be filed with the proper state office. If the document is not filed or is improperly filed, the limited partner could be treated as a general partner and, thus, lose the protection of limited liability. In addition, the limited partner must refrain from becoming involved in the day-to-day operation of the partnership. Otherwise, the limited partner might be found to be actively participating in the business, and thereby held to be a general partner with unlimited personal liability.

Limited partnership is a convenient business form for securing needed economic backers who wish to share in the profits of an enterprise without undue exposure to personal liability when a corporation may not be appropriate, or when the business does not meet all the requirements to be an S corporation (discussed later in this chapter). A limited partnership can be used to attract investment when credit is hard to get or too expensive. In return for investing, the limited partner may receive a designated share of the profits. From the entrepreneur's point of view, this may be an attractive way to fund a business, since the limited partner receives nothing if there are no profits; whereas, had the entrepreneur borrowed money from a creditor, he or she would be at risk to repay the loan regardless of the success or failure of the business.

Another use of the limited partnership is to facilitate reorganization of a general partnership after the death or retirement of a general partner. A partnership, remember, can be terminated when any partner requests it. Although the original partnership is thus technically dissolved when one partner retires, it is not uncommon for the remaining partners to agree to buy out the retiring partner's share—that is, to return that person's capital contribution and keep the business going. Raising enough cash to buy out the retiring partner, however, could jeopardize the business by forcing the remaining partners to liquidate certain partnership assets. A convenient way to avoid such a detrimental liquidation is for the retiree to step into a limited partner status. Thus, he or she can continue to share in the profits, which, to some extent, flow from that partner's past labor, while removing personal assets from the risk of partnership liabilities. In the meantime, the remaining partners are afforded the opportunity to restructure the partnership funding under more favorable conditions.

What You Don't Want: Unintended Partners

Whether yours is a straightforward partnership or a limited partnership, one arrangement you want to avoid is the unintended partnership. This can occur when you collaborate on a work with another person and your relationship is not described formally in a written agreement. Thus, if you do the photography for a corporate report, and ask a friend to provide supplementary photographs, it is essential for you to spell out in detail the arrangements between you and the other person. If you do not, you could find that the other photographer is your partner and entitled to half of the income you receive even though the contribution was minimal. You can avoid this by making an outright purchase of the other person's work or pay that person a percentage of what you are paid. Whichever arrangement you choose, you will be well advised to have a detailed written agreement prepared by an experienced business lawyer.

The Corporation

The word *corporation* may bring to mind a vision of a large company with hundreds or thousands of employees—an impersonal monster wholly alien to the world of the photographer. In fact, there is nothing in the nature of a corporation itself that requires it to be large or impersonal. In many states, even one person can incorporate a business. There are advantages and disadvantages to incorporating; if it appears advantageous to incorporate, you will find it can be done with surprising ease and with little expense. However, you will need a lawyer's assistance to ensure compliance with state formalities, instruction on corporate mechanics, and advice on corporate taxation

Differences Between a Corporation and Partnership

In describing the corporate form, it is useful to compare it to a partnership. Perhaps the most important difference is that, like limited partners, the owners of the corporation—commonly known as shareholders or stockholders—are not personally liable for the corporation's debts; they stand to lose only their investment. But unlike a limited partner, a shareholder is allowed full participation in the control of the corporation through the shareholders' voting privileges: the higher the percentage of outstanding shares owned, the more significant the control.

For the small corporation, however, limited liability may be something of an illusion because very often creditors will require that the owners either personally co-sign or guarantee any credit extended. In addition, individuals remain responsible for their wrongful acts; thus, a photographer who infringes a copyright or creates a defamatory work will remain personally liable even if incorporated. However, the corporate liability shield does protect a photographer in situations where a contract is breached if the other contracting party has agreed to look only to the corporation for responsibility. For example, publishing contracts frequently require photographers to make certain guarantees and statements of fact. If the publisher will contract with the photographer's corporation, rather than with the photographer as an individual, then the corporation alone will be liable if there is a breach.

The corporate shield also offers protection in situations where an employee of the photographer has committed a wrongful act while working for the photographer's corporation. If, for example, an assistant negligently injures a pedestrian while the assistant is driving to the store to pick up some film for the photographer, the assistant will be liable for the wrongful act and the corporation may be liable, but the photographer who owns the corporation probably will not be personally liable.

The second major difference between a corporation and a partnership relates to continuity of existence. The many events that can cause the dissolution of a partnership do not have the same effect on a corporation. In fact, it is common for perpetual existence to be established in the Articles of Incorporation. Unlike partners, shareholders cannot decide to withdraw and demand a return of capital from the corporation; all they may do is sell their stock. Therefore, a corporation may have both legal and economic continuity. But this can also be a disadvantage to shareholders or their heirs if they want to sell their stock when there are no buyers for it. However, there are agreements which may be used to guarantee a return of capital should the shareholder die or wish to withdraw.

The third difference relates to transferability of ownership. No one can become a partner without unanimous consent of the other partners unless otherwise agreed in the partnership agreement. In a corporation, however, shareholders can generally sell their shares, or any number of them. to whomever they wish. If the owners of a small corporation do not want to be open to outside ownership, transferability can be restricted.

The fourth difference is in the structure of management and control. Shareholders are given a vote in proportion to their ownership in the corporation. Other kinds of stock can be created with or without voting rights. A voting shareholder uses the vote to elect a board of directors and to create rules under which the board will operate.

The basic rules of the corporation are stated in the articles of incorporation, which are filed with the state. These serve as a sort of constitution and can be amended by shareholder vote. More detailed operational rules—bylaws—should also be prepared. Shareholders and, in many states, directors may have the power to create or amend bylaws. This varies from state to state and may be determined by the shareholders themselves. The board of directors then makes operational decisions for the corporation and might delegate day-to-day control to a president.

A shareholder, even one who owns all the stock, may not preempt a decision of the board of directors. If the board has exceeded the powers granted it by the articles or bylaws, any shareholder can sue for a court order remedying the situation. But if the board is acting within its powers, the shareholders have no recourse except formally to remove the board or any board member. In a few more-progressive states, a small corporation may entirely forego having a board of directors. In such cases, the corporation is authorized to allow the shareholders to vote on business decisions just as in a partnership.

The fifth distinction between a partnership and a corporation is the greater variety of means available to the corporation for raising additional capital. Partnerships are quite restricted in this regard; they can borrow money or, if all the partners agree, they can take on additional partners. A corporation, on the other hand, may issue more stock, and this stock can be of many different varieties: recallable at a set price, for example, or convertible into another kind of stock.

A means frequently used to attract a new investor is the issuance of preferred stock. The corporation agrees to pay the preferred shareholder some predetermined amount, known as a dividend preference, before it pays any dividends to other shareholders. It also means that, if the corporation should go bankrupt, the preferred shareholder generally will be paid out of the proceeds of liquidation before the other shareholders, known as "common shareholders," although after the corporation's creditors are paid.

The issuance of new stock merely requires, in most cases, approval by a majority of the existing shareholders. In addition, corporations can borrow money on a short-term basis by issuing notes, or for a longer period, by using long-term debt instruments known as issuing debentures or bonds. In fact, a corporation's ability to raise additional capital is limited only by its lawyer's creativity and the economics of the marketplace.

The last distinction between a partnership and a corporation discussed here is the manner in which a corporation is taxed. Under both state and federal laws the profits of the corporation are taxed to the corporation before they are paid out as dividends. Then, because the dividends constitute income to the shareholders, they are taxed again as personal income. This double taxation constitutes the major disadvantage of incorporating.

Avoiding Double Taxation of Corporate Income

There are several methods of avoiding double taxation. First, a corporation can plan its business so as not to show very much profit. This can be done by drawing off what would be profit in payments to shareholders for a variety of services. For example, a shareholder can be paid a salary, rent for property leased to the corporation, or interest on a loan made to the corporation. All of these are legal deductions from the corporate income.

The corporation can also get larger deductions for the various health and retirement benefits provided for its employees than can an individual (sole proprietorship) or a partnership. For example, a corporation can deduct all of its payments made for an employee health plan while the employees pay no personal income tax on this benefit. Sole proprietors or partnerships can deduct only a portion of these expenses.

The corporation can also reinvest its profits for reasonable business expansion. This undistributed money is not taxed as income to the shareholder, although the corporation must pay corporate tax on it. By contrast, the retained earnings of a partnership are taxed to the individual partners even though the money is not distributed. Corporate reinvestment has two advantages. First, the business can be built up with money that has been taxed only at the corporate level and on which no individual shareholder needs to pay any tax. Second, within reasonable limits, the corporation can delay the distribution of corporate earnings until a time of lower personal income of the shareholder and, thus, lower personal tax.

The S Corporation

Congress has created a hybrid organizational form that allows the owners of a small corporation to take advantage of many of the features described above but to be taxed in a manner similar to a partnership and avoid the double-taxation problem. This form of organization is called an S corporation. If the corporation meets certain requirements, which many small businesses do, the owners can elect to be taxed in a manner similar to a partnership.

In order for a corporation to qualify as an S corporation, it may not have more than thirty-five owners, who must be human beings or certain kinds of trusts. The owners must be U.S. citizens and there cannot be more than one class of stock. S corporations are generally taxed the same as partnerships, although there are some differences. Generally speaking, the shareholder/owner of an S corporation can be taxed on his or her pro rata share of the distributable profits and may deduct his or her share of distributable losses. This can be particularly advantageous in the early years of a corporation because the owners of an S corporation can deduct almost all of the losses of the corporation from their personal income, whereas they cannot do that in a standard, or C, corporation. They can have this favorable tax situation while simultaneously enjoying the corporation's limited-liability status.

C corporations are taxable entities and pay taxes on corporate earnings. In addition, shareholders who are paid dividends, pay taxes on those distributions. There is, therefore, the possibility of having dividend income taxed twice. C corporations also have higher tax rates on earnings in excess of one hundred thousand dollars.

Precautions for Minority Shareholders

Dissolving a corporation is not only painful because of certain tax penalties; it is almost always impossible without the consent of the majority of the shareholders. If you are involved in the formation of a corporation and will be a minority shareholder, you must realize that the majority will have ultimate and absolute control unless minority shareholders take certain precautions from the start. There are numerous horror stories of what some majority shareholders have done to minority shareholders. Avoiding these problems is no more difficult than drafting an agreement among the shareholders. I recommend that you retain your own attorney to represent you during the corporation's formation rather than waiting until it is too late.

Limited Liability Companies

There is a relatively new business form which may now be used in some states and is being considered in many others. Limited liability companies, or LLCs, as they are known, combine the limited liability features of a corporation with all of the tax advantages available to partnerships. Thus, a photographer conducting business through an LLC can shield his or her personal assets from the risks of the business for all situations except the individual's own wrongful acts. This liability shield is identical to that which is available for one who conducts business in the corporate form.

As previously discussed in this chapter, there is a provision in the tax law for certain qualifying corporations which will enable the shareholder/owners of those corporations to avoid the double taxation of dividends. The so-called S corporation is intended to provide small businesses with a vehicle by which the owners can avoid the double taxation of dividends. "Small corporations," as used in the tax law, does not refer to the amount of business generated; rather, it refers to the number of owners. Unfortunately, the tax rules for S corporations are not as simple as they are for partnerships. There is, thus, some difference between the tax treatment accorded an S corporation and that which is available for partnerships.

LLCs do not have the same restrictions imposed on S corporations regarding the number of owners, their citizenship, and whether they must be human beings. In fact, corporations, partnerships, and other business forms can own interests in LLCs. LLCs also may have more than one class of stock. This business form, therefore, truly combines the liability shield of the corporation with the pass-through features of a partnership (see pages 97–98).

There is, however, a restriction which is imposed on the transferability of the ownership interests in the LLC. This means that this business form may not be as desirable for big businesses as is the corporation or limited partnership.

There are some other features of the LLC which should be considered before adopting this business form. To begin with, it is new and, thus, there is virtually no case law interpreting the meaning of the new statutes. Currently, only a handful of states permit the creation of these business entities and many states do not recognize the limited liability feature of LLCs, even if validly created in another jurisdiction, when they conduct business in those states. In fact, some states will not allow LLCs to do business within their borders. It is safe to create an LLC only for the purpose of doing business in a state which recognizes that business form or in another state recognizing the LLC as such.

It is important for you as a business person to determine which business form will be most advantageous for you. This can best be done by consulting an experienced business lawyer and having your situation evaluated.

THE TAX CONSEQUENCES OF BUSINESS ORGANIZATION

Prior to the 1986 Tax Reform Act, beneficial tax treatment was the primary impetus behind many professionals' choice to incorporate rather than creating a partnership or remaining sole proprietors. Individual tax rates were as high as seventy percent, while the top corporate rate was around thirty-four percent—a major tax shelter for those who were able to incorporate. The 1986 Act reduced individual rates to levels equal or below corporate rates.

Four years earlier, the Tax Equity and Fiscal Responsibility Act (TEFRA) took away one of the other primary advantages of incorporation. Prior to the act, corporate shareholders benefitted from the ability to invest a greater amount of income in tax-deferred retirement plans than persons in partnerships or sole proprietorships. TEFRA, in effect, leveled the playing field, so that the choice of business form would not be influenced by variations in tax treatment of retirement plans.

Although the tax benefits between the various business organizations have been roughly equalized, there are still some differences with respect to the tax treatment of the various entities.

Sole Proprietorships
As with S corporations and partnerships, a sole proprietorship's income and deductions pass through to the "sole proprietor" and are reported on his or her individual income tax return. Even though the business form is labeled "sole proprietorship," the practitioner may employ several other practitioners on a salaried basis without affecting his or her personal tax treatment.

Partnerships
Partnerships are taxed in much the same way as S corporations—business income (and deductions) pass directly through to the individual partners. With certain exceptions, each partner's distributable share is taxed at his or her individual income tax rate. There are, however, more technical rules which apply to different situations. Since partnership tax is a very complicated body of law, if you choose this business form, it is recommended that you consult with an accountant.

Corporations
As was discussed in chapter 6, there are two types of corporations—the "C" corporation and the "S" corporation. The designation "professional corporation" does not impact the tax characterization. The professional C corporation is regarded as a separate legal entity. It is, therefore, taxed as a separate entity. All corporate income is taxed at the corporate rate (thirty-five percent for professional service corporations as of the date of this writing), and then again at the shareholder level when it is distributed as dividends. One might think that this shareholder-level tax could be avoided, or at least postponed, by causing the corporation to retain its earnings instead of paying them out. But Congress has dealt with this possible abuse through the imposition of an "accumulated earnings tax."

The accumulated earnings tax is a 39.6% "penalty tax" which is imposed on all "accumulated earnings"—earnings the IRS treats as dividends which should have been distributed. Accumulated earnings are defined as earnings in excess of reasonable business needs. If the accumulation can be justified (for example, to allow for an anticipated and legitimate expansion of your business), then the tax likely will not be imposed. There are additional ways to avoid this tax which should be discussed with your tax advisor if you perceive the possibility of liability.

It is the "two-tier" tax—once at the corporate level and again at the shareholder level—that dissuades many small businesses from opting for C corporation status. There are methods of reducing the shareholder tax, using the maximum allowable deductions (as will be discussed later in this chapter). Most small businesses elect to be treated as an S corporation and thereby eliminate the double tax.

In order to be taxed as an S corporation, a special election must be made and filed with the IRS. In addition, certain requirements must be met: There may be no more than thirty-five shareholders; there may not be shareholders who are "non-individuals" (except certain estates and trusts), such as another corporation; there may not be nonresident aliens as shareholders; and the corporation may not have more than one class of stock.

S corporations avoid double taxation because corporate income "passes through" directly to the shareholders. There is no "trap" of corporate earnings at the corporate level. Each shareholder must recognize a proportionate amount of corporate income directly on his or her individual income tax return, which is taxed at individual income tax rates. That means a tax savings of 4.6% for individuals in the highest income bracket (assuming a flat corporate rate of 35% and individual rate of 39.6%). Most of the standard business deductions that are applicable to the C corporation are also applicable to the S corporation. The shareholders utilize the business deductions themselves, in proportion to their ownership. Such deductions can, however, be used only to offset business profits, not unrelated income.

Limited Liability Companies

As was discussed in the previous chapter, Limited Liability Companies (LLCs) combine the limited liability features of a corporation with all of the tax advantages available to partnerships. LLCs enjoy all of the tax pass-through features of a partnership. The technical tax rules have been liberalized in connection with this business form and the owners of an LLC can enjoy all of the tax pass-through features accorded partners in a partnership.

Employee Compensation

For photographers who have chosen to do business as C corporations, payment of employee compensation is actually one of the most effective ways to minimize or eliminate double taxation. Rather than paying out corporate earnings to shareholder-employees as non-deductible dividends, the corporation can pay out high salaries and then receive a business expense deduction for the wages paid.

Although an S corporation is not saddled with the double tax, the corporation (shareholders) still benefits from a deduction for employee compensation, since it results in a decrease in taxable income.

It should be apparent that this deduction provides a potentially large loophole in the tax law. Congress and the courts have all but closed this loophole by placing a limit upon the amount that may be deducted as a business expense—only that which is "reasonable compensation" may be deducted.

A corporation cannot avoid income tax by paying excessive salaries to the stockholder-employees. The IRS frequently audits closely-held corporations for this type of abuse. Although most challenges are to salaries and benefits for stockholders, excessive compensation paid to a non-stockholder employee also has been successfully challenged by the Service.

Reasonability, as always, depends on all the circumstances of the particular case. Factors that the courts have considered include the nature of the job, the size and complexity of the business, prevailing rates of compensation, the company's profitability, the uniqueness of the employee's skills or experience, the number of hours worked, the employee's salary as compared with the salaries of co-workers, general economic conditions and the presence, absence, and amount of dividends paid.

If a salary is found excessive, no deduction will be allowed for the part of the payment that is excessive. Even though the employer cannot deduct the full amount paid, the employee must report and pay tax on the full amount received.

Usually, a new business is more concerned with underpayment than over-compensation. Employees may work long, hard hours with little compensation in the hope of a brighter future. The Service realizes this. In later years, when the business is profitable, employees can be compensated for the underpayment of former years by additions to their salaries. The base salaries must be reasonable and the additional amounts also must be reasonable in light of the past services performed and the compensation already received.

Compensation also may be fixed as a percentage of profits or earnings. Contingent plans of this nature may result in low salaries in lean years and above-average salaries in good years. The Service accepts this too, as long as, on the average, the salaries are not unreasonable. Of course, some premium is reasonable due to the risk assumed by the employee who accepts such a plan.

Contingent plans are suspect, however, when used for owner-employees since they can be used to avoid dividends in good years. A stockholder-employee's reward for an increase in business should be a reasonable salary and increased dividends.

Statutory Benefit Plans

Statutory, tax-exempt benefit plans, that is, plans which are specified in the Internal Revenue Code, are available for accident and health coverage, group term life insurance, profit sharing, pension, and contributory savings plans, to name a few. These plans are not limited to corporate employers. The requirements for benefit plans are extremely complex from a tax standpoint, and retirement plans must also comply with ERISA, the federal Employee Retirement Income Security Act.

Even though the myriad rules and regulations are tedious, the plans are worth consideration. If a plan conforms to the rules, employer contributions are immediately deductible as business expenses but are not taxable to the employees as income. Employees are taxed only when they receive payments from the pension plan. Even more important, in the case of retirement plans no tax is imposed on the investment growth of funds deposited in the plan.

Statutory benefit plans can provide accident, medical, or group-term life insurance, educational assistance, legal services, or child care. Each is covered by separate rules and requirements, but all plans must meet a common set of rules to be tax exempt.

Generally, structuring plans to favor highly compensated employees will subject the employees to tax liability on those benefits. This is a complex area and you should consult with your tax adviser or accountant before adopting any of these plans.

A statutory plan also must meet a benefits requirement so that the average benefit received by non-highly compensated employees must equal or exceed seventy-five percent of the average benefits received by highly-compensated employees under the same or similar plans.

A "highly-compensated employee" is an employee who owns five percent of the business, or receives compensation in excess of $75,000 annually, or receives over $50,000 and is in the highest paid group of employees for the year, or is an officer and receives more than $45,000 in compensation annually. These numbers are in effect as of the date of this writing but are indexed annually to reflect inflation.

In determining the required eligibility percentages, the following employees may be excluded: temporary and part-time employees, employees who are under twenty-one years old, employees covered by collective bargaining agreements (unions), employees who are nonresident aliens and who receive no U.S. taxable income, and employees who have been on the job less than one year (six months in the case of medical benefits).

Following is a sketchy review of some statutory plans:

- An employer may provide up to $50,000 of tax-free, group-term life insurance for each employee. Premiums on coverage exceeding $50,000 in face amount are taxable to employees, unless the employee contributes to the plan with his or her own taxable income.

- An employee may receive up to $5,250 in tax-free educational assistance per year from a funded educational-assistance program.

In addition, contributions by employers to health and accident plans are generally tax exempt only if they provide continuing extensions of coverage for various specified time periods after termination of employment.

When an employee receives payment for medical expenses, the amount received is not taxable income unless the employee is already receiving compensation from another source or takes an income tax deduction for the medical expenses.

The employee is also not taxed on amounts received to compensate for injury due to permanent loss of use of a body part or function or permanent disfigurement.

Amounts received to compensate an employee for loss of income due to illness or injury are taxable as income.

A plan can provide assistance for child or other dependent care. The aggregate amount excluded from the employee's income cannot exceed $45,000 in the case of a single parent or marital unit. If an employee receives $2,500 of tax-free child care assistance, the spouse is eligible to receive only an additional $2,500 in tax-free assistance.

Qualified Plans. Retirement benefits may be provided under "qualified plans." The rules for qualified pension, profit sharing, and stock bonus plans are too numerous to summarize.

Eligibility and benefit rules exist to ensure nondiscrimination. Since it is reasonable to allow for different employer contribution amounts to various plans based upon an employee's value and years of service, there are special rules to prevent and remedy top-heavy plans where accumulated contributions on behalf of highly-compensated employees exceed those for other employees.

These plans must be separately funded and administered under rules designed to guarantee, to the extent possible, that retirement funds cannot be reached, tampered with, squandered, or mismanaged by the employer.

There are also vesting requirements so that employees can rely on the plans without worrying about forfeiture due to excessively long employment-period requirements. Maintenance of a qualified plan is impossible without specialized professional help.

Cafeteria Plans. Cafeteria plans have nothing to do with employee lunch rooms. Under a cafeteria plan, an employer may set up a "menu" whereby an employee is allotted a certain amount of benefit credit and allowed to choose between various amounts and combinations of plans or the receipt of additional taxable income. Amounts allocable to elected benefit plans are not taxable to the employee. In this way, an employee can tailor a benefits program to best meet his or her individual circumstances. Fringe benefits and educational assistance plans may not be included in cafeteria plans.

Fringe Benefits. Certain fringe benefits may be provided tax free to employees. Such benefits might include employee discounts, subsidized cafeterias, parking facilities, on-site athletic facilities, etc. Generally, these benefits must be of no additional cost to the employer, or be worth so little that the administrative cost of keeping track of them exceeds the value of the benefit.

Shareholder employees of C corporations can take advantage of all of the above fringe benefits as employees. S corporation shareholders generally cannot avail themselves of certain fringe benefits such as cafeteria plans, fully deductible health insurance at the corporate level, dependent care plans, or group term life plans.

Keeping Taxes Low

Photographers rarely think of themselves as being engaged in a business; many, in fact, go to great lengths to avoid feeling involved in the world of commerce. The IRS, however, treats the professional photographer like anyone else in business; thus the photographer has many of the same tax concerns as any other business person. In addition, most photographers have some special tax problems.

First, most professional photographers do not work for a fixed wage or salary; as a result, a photographer's income can fluctuate radically from one tax year to the next. (This is true too, of course, for the photographer who works for someone else but also freelances.) Second, many tax rules designed to facilitate investment are not useful to photographers. Photographers can, however, benefit from certain provisions of the Internal Revenue Code to reduce their income tax liability.

Record-keeping

In order to take advantage of all the tax laws that are favorable to you, it is imperative that you keep good business records. The Internal Revenue Service does not require that you keep any particular type of records. It will be satisfied so long as your record-keeping clearly reflects your income and is consistent over time so that it can make accurate comparisons from year to year when evaluating your income.

The first step in keeping business records that will allow you to maximize your deductions is to open a checking account for your business. Try to pay all your business expenses by check. Be sure to fill in the amount, date, and reason for each check on the stub. If the check was written for an expense related to a particular client or job, be sure to put the client's name or a job number on both the check and the stub. Finally, keep all of your cancelled checks.

Second, file for a taxpayer identification number. In most states and in some cities, photography is a business subject to sales tax. You will need to get in touch with your state and city sales tax bureaus to ascertain their requirements. Usually, the bureau will issue you a taxpayer identification number after you fill out some forms. Then you can buy certain equipment and supplies without paying the sales tax. However, you will later have to act as an agent of the state, collecting sales tax from your clients and paying it to the state. You should be aware that even if you do not collect the sales tax from your customers, you will be liable for paying it.

Third, keep an expense diary which is similar in form to a date book. You should use your expense diary on a daily basis, noting all cash outlays, such as business-related cab fare, tolls, tips, emergency supplies, as they occur. This will satisfy the IRS requirement that you have both a receipt and good evidence of the business purpose for any expenses greater than twenty-five dollars.

Qualifying for Business Deductions

There are two principal ways of reducing tax liability. First, there are significant deductions available to photographers. Second, as I will discuss later in this chapter, photographers can spread their taxable income (and thus reduce their tax liability) by using different provisions in the tax code.

Professional photographers may deduct their business expenses and thereby significantly reduce their taxable income. However, as with other artists and craftspeople, photographers must be able to establish that they are engaged in a trade or business and not merely a personal hobby. You must keep full and accurate records. Receipts are a necessity. Furthermore, it would be best if you had, in addition to a separate checking account, a complete set of books for all of the activities of your trade or business. A dilettante is not entitled to trade or business deductions.

Tax laws presume that a photographer is engaged in a business or trade, as opposed to a hobby, if a net profit results from the photography during three out of the five consecutive years ending with the taxable year in question. If the photographer has not had three profitable years in the last five, the IRS may contend that the photographer is merely indulging in a hobby, in which case the photographer will have to prove *profit motive* in order to claim business expenses. Proof of profit motive does not require the photographer to prove that there was some chance a profit would actually be made; it requires proof only that the photographer intended to make a profit.

The Treasury Regulations call for an objective standard on the profit-motive issue, so statements of the photographer as to intent will not suffice as proof. The regulations list nine factors to be used in determining profit motive:

- The manner in which the taxpayer carries on the activity (i.e., effective business routines and bookkeeping procedures);
- The expertise of the taxpayer or the taxpayer's advisors (i.e., taking courses in appropriate subjects, awards, prior sales or exhibitions, critical recognition, membership in professional organizations, etc.);
- The time and effort expended in carrying on the activity (i.e., at least several hours a day, preferably on a regular basis);
- Expectation that business assets will increase in value (a factor that is of little relevance to the photographer);
- The success of the taxpayer in similar or related activities (i.e., past successes, either financial or critical, even if prior to the relevant five-year period);
- History of income or losses with respect to the activity (i.e., increases in receipts from year to year unless losses vastly exceed receipts over a long period of time);
- The amount of profits, if any, which are earned;
- Financial status (wealth sufficient to support a hobby would weigh against the profit motive);
- Elements of personal pleasure or recreation (i.e., if significant traveling is involved and few photographs produced, the court may be suspicious of profit motive).

No single factor will determine the results. The case of *Young* v. *United States* provides an example of how the factors are used. Young was a psychoanalyst who also had a photography business. Although Young was not a commercial photographer and she had had large, serious losses, the court held that she had a genuine profit motive in pursuing photography. The court was influenced by the fact that Young did not appear to be pursuing the occupation of photography for mere pleasure or social prestige and that she was organized as a business and kept conventional business records.

Deductible Expenses

Once you have established yourself as engaged in photography as a business, many of your ordinary and necessary expenditures for professional photography are deductible business expenses. This would include photographic equipment and supplies, office equipment, research or professional books and magazines, travel for business purposes, certain conference fees, agent commissions, postage, legal fees, accounting fees, and work space. Work space as a deductible expense—particularly space in one's home, which is a matter of concern to numerous business people including photographers—is covered in the next chapter.

Most of a photographer's expenses are classified as *current expenses*: items with a useful life of less than one year. For example, film and supplies, postage, modeling fees, and telephone bills would be current expenses. These expenses are fully deductible in the year incurred.

There are some business expenses, however, that cannot be fully deducted in the year of purchase but must be depreciated or amortized. These costs are *capital expenditures*. For example, the cost of professional equipment such as a camera or lighting equipment, which have a useful life of more than one year, are capital expenditures and cannot be fully deducted in the year of purchase. Instead, the taxpayer has to depreciate, or allocate, the cost of the item over the estimated useful life of the asset. This is sometimes referred to as *capitalizing* or amortizing the cost. Although the actual useful life of professional equipment will vary, fixed periods have been established in the code over which depreciation may be deducted.

In some cases it may be difficult to decide whether an expense is a capital expenditure or a current expense. Repairs to equipment are one example. If you spend $200 servicing a camera, this expense may or may not constitute a capital expenditure. The general test is whether the amount spent restoring the equipment has added to its value or substantially prolonged its useful life. Since the cost of replacing short-lived parts of equipment to keep it in efficient working condition does not substantially add to the useful life of equipment, such a cost would be a current cost and would be deductible. The cost of reconditioning equipment, on the other hand, significantly extends its useful life. Thus, such a cost is a capital expenditure and be depreciated.

For many small businesses, an immediate deduction can be taken when equipment is purchased. Up to $17,500 of such purchases may be "expensed" each year, and need not be depreciated at all. This is called the "election to depreciate certain business assets." In order to take advantage of the provision, you must have net income of at least the amount of the deduction.

Commissions paid to agents, as well as fees paid to lawyers or accountants for business purposes, are generally deductible as current expenses. The same is true of salaries paid to assistants and others whose services are necessary for the photography business. If you need to hire help, it is a good idea to hire people on an individual-project basis as independent contractors rather than as regular employees. This way, you do not have to pay for social security, disability, and withholding tax. You should specify the job-by-job basis of the assignments and detail when each project is to be completed, and, if possible, allow the person you are hiring to choose the place to do the work. There may be other restrictions when attempting to characterize an individual as an independent contractor; you should discuss this with your attorney or tax adviser.

Business Use of An Automobile

If you or your employees use personal vehicles for business, an amount proportionate with the business use may qualify for depreciation, maintenance, and operating expense deductions. You must keep accurate records of the number of "business miles" driven, and of the time, place, and purpose of the travel. If records are not kept, no deduction will be allowed. The records must establish total annual mileage, commuting mileage, business mileage, percentage of business use, and the date the vehicle was placed in service. This information must be reported on the tax return. You will also be asked to indicate whether there is written evidence to support the claimed use of the vehicle for business. If the vehicle is a "luxury" vehicle, there are special rules that apply for depreciation purposes.

If an automobile is used solely for business, records separating business from personal use are not necessary if certain conditions are met: (1) the vehicle is leased or owned by the employer and provided to one or more employees for use in connection with the business; (2) the vehicle is kept at the employer's premises when not in use and no employee using the vehicle lives at the employer's address; and (3) a written policy of the employer forbids personal use of the vehicle, and the vehicle is not used personally except for minor deviations such as lunch stops while on the road for business purposes.

Travel, Entertainment, and Conventions

Many photographers travel abroad in order to shoot certain subjects. Even more commonly, a photographer might travel in the U.S.

On a business trip, whether within the U.S. or abroad, ordinary and necessary expenses, including travel and lodging, may be one-hundred percent deductible if your travel is solely for business purposes, except for luxury water travel. Note, however, only fifty percent of the costs of business meals, and meals consumed while on a business trip, are deductible. If the trip primarily involves a personal vacation, you can deduct business-related expenses at the destination, but you may not deduct the transportation costs.

If the trip is primarily for business, but part of the time is given to a personal vacation, you must indicate which expenses are for business and which for pleasure. This is *not* true in the case of foreign trips if one of the following exceptions applies:

- You had no control over arranging the trip,
- The trip outside of the U.S. was for a week or less,
- You are not a managing executive or shareholder of the company that employed you.

If you are claiming one of these exceptions you should be careful to have supporting documentation. If you cannot take advantage of one of the exceptions, then you must allocate expenses for the trip abroad according to the percentage of the trip devoted to business (as opposed to vacation).

Whether inside or outside of the U.S., the definition of what constitutes a business day can be very helpful to the taxpayer in determining a trip's deductibility. Travel days, including the day of departure and the day of return, count as business days if business activities occurred on such days. If travel is outside the U.S., the same rules apply if the foreign trip is for more than seven days. Any day which the taxpayer spends on business counts as a business day even if only a part of the day is spent on business. A day in which business is canceled through no fault of the taxpayer counts as a business day. Saturdays, Sundays, and holidays count as business days even though no business is conducted, provided that business is conducted on the Friday before and the Monday after the weekend, or one day on either side of the holiday.

Entertainment expenses incurred for the purpose of developing an existing business are also deductible, in the amount of fifty percent of the actual cost. However, you must be especially careful about recording entertainment expenses. You should record in your logbook the amount, date, place, type of entertainment, business purpose, substance of the discussion, the participants in the discussion, and the business relationship of the parties who are being entertained. Keep receipts for any expenses over twenty-five dollars. You should also keep in mind the new stipulation in the tax code which disallows deductibility for expenses which are "lavish or extravagant under the circumstances." No guidelines have yet been developed as to the definition of "lavish or extravagant," but you should be aware of the restriction nevertheless. If tickets to a sporting, cultural, or other event are purchased, only the face value of the ticket is allowed as a deduction. If a skybox or other luxury box seat is purchased or leased and is used for business entertaining, the maximum deduction now allowed is the cost of a non-luxury box seat.

The above rules cover business travel and entertainment expenses both inside and outside of the United States. The rules are more stringent for deducting expenses incurred while attending conventions and conferences outside the United States. Also, the IRS tends to review very carefully any deductions for attendance at business seminars that also involve a family vacation, whether inside the U.S. or abroad. In order to deduct the business expense, the taxpayer must be able to show, with documents, that the reason for attending the meeting was to promote production of income. Normally, for a spouse's expenses to be deductible, the spouse's presence must be required by the photographer's employer. In the case of an independent photographer who has organized into a partnership or small corporation, it is wise, if the spouse will also be going on business trips, to make the spouse a partner, employee, or member of the board of the company. Often, seminars will offer special activities for husbands and wives that will provide documentation later on.

As a general rule, the business deductions are allowed for conventions and seminars held in North America. The IRS is taking a closer look at cruise-ship seminars and is now requiring two statements to be attached to the tax return when such seminars are involved. The first statement substantiates the number of days on the ship, the number of hours spent each day on business, and the activities in the program. The second statement must come from the sponsor of the convention to verify the first information. In addition, the ship must be registered in the U.S., and all ports of call must be located in the U.S. or its possessions. Again, the key for the taxpayer taking this sort of deduction is careful documentation and substantiation.

Keeping a logbook or expense diary is probably the best line of defense for the photographer with respect to business expenses incurred while traveling. If you are on the road, keep these things in mind:

With respect to travel expenses:
- Keep proof of the costs,
- Record the time of departure,
- Record the number of days spent on business,
- List the places visited and the business purposes of your activities.

With respect to the transportation costs:
- Keep copies of all receipts in excess of tewnty-five dollars,
- If traveling by car, keep track of mileage, and
- Log all other expenses in your diary.

Similarly, with meals, tips, and lodging, keep receipts for all items over twenty-five dollars make sure to record all less-expensive items in your logbook.

Photographers may also take tax deductions for their attendance at workshops, seminars, retreats, and the like, provided that they are careful to document the business nature of the trip. Accurate record-keeping is the first line of defense for tax preparation. Note that it is no longer possible to deduct for investment seminars or conventions (as opposed to business conventions).

Charitable Deductions

The law provides that an individual or business can donate either money or property to qualified charities and take a tax deduction for the donation. Individuals are afforded more favorable deductions for donations of money or property they own than are photographers donating their own work or business people who donate property out of their inventory. Since this area can be quite technical, you should consult with your tax adviser before making any charitable donations. In addition, there have been some abuses on the part of charities that resulted in misappropriation of donated funds. If you have any question about the validity of a particular charity, you should contact your state Attorney General's Office or the local governmental agency that polices charitable solicitations in your area.

Charitable donations of work by the creator such as a photographer donating his or her own prints or negatives will entitle the taxpayer to deduct for federal income tax purposes only the cost of the materials donated, i.e., film and developing rather than the fair market value of the donation. Some states, such as Oregon and Maine, have enacted laws which allow the taxpayer to deduct more from state income taxes when charitable donations are made to qualified charities.

Grants, Prizes, and Awards

Those photographers who receive income from grants or fellowships should be aware that this income can be excluded from gross income and thus represents considerable tax savings. To qualify for this exclusion the grant must be for the purpose of furthering the photographer's education and training. Amounts received under a grant or fellowship that are specifically designated to cover related expenses for the purpose of the grant are no longer fully deductible. Furthermore, if the grant is given as compensation for services or is primarily for the benefit of the grant-giving organization, it cannot be excluded.

For scholarships and fellowships granted after August 16, 1986, the above deductions are allowed only if the recipient is a degree candidate. The amount of the exclusion from income is limited to the amounts used for tuition, fees, books, supplies, and equipment. Amounts designated for room, board, and other incidental expenses are considered to be income. No exclusions from income are allowed for recipients who are not degree candidates.

The above rules apply to income from grants and fellowships. Unfortunately, the Tax Reform Act of 1986 also put tighter restrictions on money, goods, or services received as prizes or awards. Previously, the amounts received for certain awards were excluded from income in certain cases where the recipient was rewarded for past achievements, and had not applied for the award. Examples of this type of award are the Pulitzer Prize or the Nobel Prize. Under the present law, any prizes or awards for religious, charitable, scientific, or artistic achievements are included as income to the recipient, unless the prize is assigned to charity. If you do not know whether a particular activity is deductible, you should consult with a competent CPA or tax adviser before embarking on it.

Income in Installments and Deferred Payments

In addition to taking all possible deductions, a photographer can spread income by receiving payment in installments. Care must be taken with the mechanics of this arrangement, however. If a photographer sells photographs for a negotiable note due in full at some future date, or for some other deferred-payment obligation that is essentially equivalent to cash or has an ascertainable fair market value, the photographer may have to report the total proceeds of the sale as income realized when the note is received, not when the note is paid off with cash. However, if you sell property and receive payments in successive tax years, the Internal Revenue Code allows you to report the income on an installment basis. Under this method, tax is imposed only as payments are received.

For example, suppose you sell a series of photographs for $3,000. Ordinarily the entire $3,000 would be taxable income in the year you received it. But if you use the installment method, with four payments of $750 plus interest received annually over four years, income from the sale will be taxed as the installments are received. In either case, the amount of income is $3,000, but under the installment method the amount is spread out over four years. This could put you in a lower tax bracket than you would have been in had you taken the full $3,000 in the year you sold your photographs.

Photographers in high tax brackets may wish to defer income until the future. To do this, a photographer could agree in a contract that payments will not exceed a certain amount in any one year, with excess payments to be carried over and paid in the future. This would result in tax savings if, when the deferred amounts are finally paid, the photographer is in a lower tax bracket.

There are drawbacks to deferred payments which include the possibility that your client may not be willing to pay interest on the deferred sums, or the possibility that the client could go broke before you are fully paid. You should consider these risks carefully before entering into a contract for deferred payments, because it might be quite difficult to change the arrangement if the need should arise.

Spreading Income Among a Family

Another strategy for photographers is to divert some of their income directly to members of their immediate family who are in lower tax brackets by hiring them as employees. Putting dependent children on the payroll can result in a substantial tax savings for professional photographers because you can deduct the salaries as a business expense, and, at the same time, you may not be required to withhold social security from the children's wages.

Your child can earn up to the amount of the standard deduction without any tax liability. You, as the taxpayer, can still claim a personal dependency exemption for the child if you provide over half of their support; however, the amount the child could earn without any tax liability would drop. This salary arrangement is permissible so long as the child is under nineteen years of age, or, if nineteen or older, is a full-time student.

The following are other restrictions on such an arrangement:
- The salary must be reasonable in relation to the child's age and the work performed
- The work performed must be a necessary service to the business
- The work must actually be performed by the child

A second method of transferring income to members of your family is the creation of a family partnership. Each partner is entitled to receive an equal share of the overall income, unless the partnership agreement provides otherwise. The income is taxed once as individual income to each partner. Thus, the photographer with a family partnership can break up and divert income to the family members so it will be taxed to them according to their respective tax brackets. The income received by children may be taxed at significantly lower rates, resulting in more income reaching the family than if it had all been received by the photographer, who is presumably in a higher tax bracket than the children.

Although the IRS allows family partnerships, it may subject them to close scrutiny to ensure that the partnership is not a sham. Unless the partnership capital is a substantial income-producing factor and unless partners are reasonably compensated for services performed on the partnership's behalf, the IRS may, in applying the section of the code which deals with distribution of partners' shares and family partnerships, decide to forbid the shift in income. This section provides that a person owning a capital interest in a family partnership will be considered a partner for tax purposes even if he or she received the capital interest as a gift. But the gift must be genuine, and it should not be revocable.

Incorporating a Family

In the past, some families incorporated in order to take advantage of the then more favorable corporate tax rates. If the IRS questioned the motivation for such an incorporation, the courts examined the intent of the family members, and if the sole purpose of incorporating was tax avoidance, the scheme was disallowed.

There may, however, be other reasons for incorporating, as, for example, to obtain limited liability as discussed in chapter 6. Similarly, for anyone who teaches photography, taking photographs may be an occupational requirement. A photographer may, therefore, wish to incorporate and elect to be taxed as an S corporation. This will enable the corporation to insulate the photographer from personal liability while permitting the business to be taxed as if it were individually owned. If the photographer employs a spouse and children, salaries paid to them will be considered business deductions and thus reduce the photographer's taxable income. When the spouse and children are made owners of the corporation by being provided with shares of stock in it, all of the benefits discussed in the preceding section on partnership will be available. Note, however, that losses derived from passive investment, such as stock ownership, may be used only to offset earnings from passive investments and may not be deducted against ordinary income.

Capital Gains Tax

Until just recently, the capital gains tax was nothing more than a relic of the past. The capital gains preference has been and still is a hot topic for partisan debate. In 1991, a modest capital gains preference was reinstated, setting a 28% tax cap on assets disposed of which produce a capital gain. For persons in the middle-to-low-income tax bracket, the capital gains tax is meaningless. But for individuals in the top (39.6%) tax bracket, it means an 11.6% tax reduction on the income realized any time an asset which produces a capital gain is disposed of.

The key to a working understanding of the capital gains tax is the definition of a "capital asset." Capital assets are items of property held by the taxpayer, often for investment purposes. The law does not clearly define a capital asset, but it does identify items which are *not* capital assets. Among other things, "capital asset" does not include property used in a trade or business which is subject to the rules for depreciation, inventory held for sale, or real property used in the trade or business. All other property held by the taxpayer is a capital asset—for example, the stock held in the incorporated practice (or any other business in which the taxpayer holds stock).

When a capital asset is sold, the net amount realized, minus the adjusted "basis" of the asset (the acquisition price minus such things as the amount of any depreciation taken against it) and selling expense, is a capital gain or loss. Capital gains or losses also result from the sale of other property besides capital assets. These exceptions will be discussed later.

Other Property Subject to Capital Gain or Loss Rules

The sale or exchange of property other than capital assets can result in a capital gain or loss. Basically, any property that can have basis can produce capital gain or loss on disposition in the right set of circumstances.

The sale of inventory does not result in a capital gain or loss even if the inventory is sold in bulk. There may be a different result if the entire practice is sold and then liquidated but, if the inventory is sold at an advertised liquidation, the taxpayer has a good argument that the inventory was sold as goods to customers, resulting in ordinary gain or loss.

Except for like-kind exchanges, the sale of real estate owned and used by a business, including long-term leaseholds, or the sale of depreciable business property, such as furniture or equipment, can result in capital gain or loss.

These are called "section 1231" gains and losses. If all the sales of section 1231 property result in a net section 1231 gain for the year, the net gain is treated as capital gain. But if section 1231 losses for the year exceed section 1231 gains, the resulting net loss is treated as ordinary loss and maybe used to offset ordinary income without limit. The rule is fairly simple for the first year in which section 1231 loss occurs. The taxpayer must keep track of his section 1231 losses, however, for the next five years following their occurrence. Each time the taxpayer uses a net 1231 loss to offset ordinary income, the amount must be dated and posted to a hypothetical "recapture account." Any section 1231 net gain occurring over the next five years must be reported as ordinary income to the extent of the amount in the recapture account. The idea is that the tax benefit gained by treating capital losses as ordinary will be erased over time by treating capital gains as ordinary income.

Thankfully, section 1231 does not apply to property held for one year or less. Sale of short-term property of this type yields ordinary income or ordinary loss.

The technicality of the capital gains tax serves to illustrate the immense complexity of the Internal Revenue Code. The code is full of pitfalls for the unwary; however, with the aid of a competent tax advisor, one can avoid these pitfalls, and hopefully reduce the "pinch" of this taxing situation.

Sales Tax

There are several state and local taxes that a photographer might be subject to, such as sales taxes, unincorporated business taxes, commercial occupancy taxes, and inventory taxes. Sales taxes do vary from state to state; therefore, be sure to find out what taxes your city and state have. Intangible property sales, such as reproduction rights, usually do not have a sales tax associated with them. Also, sales taxes customarily are levied on the last sale when the merchandise reaches the consumer; the manufacturer, distributor, and others earlier in the production chain generally do not pay sales tax. Other states require the out-of-state seller to collect tax for the state in which the goods are delivered. When selling your work across state lines, it is important to know the sales tax regulations in both states. Some states impose a sales tax when transporting goods outside of the state, while other states do not.

As a photographer, you are probably quite often selling a service (intangible goods), as well as your work (tangible goods). This can present some complicated sales tax issues, especially in light of the fact that sales tax regulations differ from state to state. When a photographer sells the reproduction rights to his work, usually there is no sales tax levied, because reproduction rights are intangible. However, in some states, if a tangible item is also sold with the intangible rights, the entire amount of the transaction will be taxed. A photographer can give a client possession of a print without the photographer having to collect sales tax, provided that the print is returned to the photographer in *exactly* the same condition as it was when it left the photographer. Otherwise, a sales tax will have to be collected.

The New York Sales Tax Bureau, for example, stipulates that when you bill a client for both a service and a tangible item, sales tax must be paid on the entire transaction, even though had the services been billed separately, they would not have been subject to tax.

You should contact your local Sales Tax Bureau and find out what the tax laws are in your city and state. If you are actually engaged in a business, in some states you can register with your local Sales Tax Bureau, and receive a resale number. That number can be used when you buy materials that you plan to resell. You also may not have to pay sales tax for equipment purchased for use in the production of your tangible work, such as photographic equipment, when your photographs will be sold.

Certain organizations such as charities and museums are customarily tax exempt. They frequently have a tax-exempt resale certificate proving their tax-exempt status. If a client claims to be tax exempt, you should insist on verification, for you, the photographer, as well as your client will be liable for any unpaid sales tax.

TAX DEDUCTIONS

FOR THE OFFICE

AT HOME

I t is quite common for photographers to have offices, studios, or darkrooms at home for a variety of reasons. The most important reason, though, is probably economic. The cost of renting a separate studio or darkroom is such that many photographers prefer to work at home. Others, of course, choose to work at home because it enables them to juggle work and family obligations.

Before 1976, you could deduct that portion of your household expenses that could reasonably be allocated to professional work. However, in 1976 Congress added Section 280A to the Internal Revenue Code. This law generally disallows any deduction for the use of your personal residence in any business. It applies not only to the building in which you the taxpayer live, but also to any structure attached to the house or on the property. There are, however, limited exceptions to the law.

Exclusive and Regular Use

You may be able to satisfy one or more of the exceptions to this rule. The first exception applies to any portion of the residence used *exclusively* and *on a regular basis* as the photographer's *principal place of business*.

The qualifications for this exception are strictly construed by the IRS and the courts. The requirement of exclusivity means that you may not mix personal use and business use. In other words, an office that doubles as a storeroom for personal belongings, a laundry room, or the like will not qualify as an office for tax purposes, and you may not deduct such space as an office.

However, there has been a recent liberalization of this rule in some parts of the country where the courts have held that a studio or an office can exist in a room that has a personal use, so long as a clearly defined area is used exclusively for business. It is important to remember that generally the Internal Revenue Service functions on a regional basis. Except for issues that have been reserved for decision by the national office, each IRS office is autonomous and makes its own decisions until the United States Supreme Court or Congress makes a decision that applies nationally. That is why the decision by a lower court in one area may not apply elsewhere.

The requirement regarding regular use means that the use of the room may not be merely incidental or occasional. Obviously, there is a gray area between regular and occasional. Perhaps some photographers can use this rule as an inducement to overcome temporary bouts of laziness or *ennui*. For if you as a photographer are planning on deducting any expenses for your office, you must keep working to satisfy the regularity test.

The Focal Point Test

Used to determine the principal place of business, the focal point test focuses on the place where services are performed and income is generated. The test requires looking at the particular facts of each case, but generally the key elements include: (1) the amount of income derived from your business done there; (2) the amount of time you spend there; and (3) the nature of the facility.

The tax court has, on one occasion, strayed from the focal point test. The court determined that a home office deduction, while not able to meet the principal place of business test, was, nevertheless, *essential* to the taxpayer's business. The deduction was allowed; however, it raised the ire of the IRS. It would not be prudent for you to rely on this liberal interpretation.

IRS Regulation 1.280-A-2(b) allows a taxpayer to have a different principal place of business for each trade or business in which that person is engaged. Thus it is now possible, for example, for a photographer doing different types of work at a studio and at home to have a different principal place of business for each photography enterprise.

Prior to a January 1993 U.S. Supreme Court ruling, the court also looked at practical necessity—self-employed individuals could deduct home-office expenses if part of their home was used exclusively for activities that were essential to their businesses. Now, however, in *Commissioner* v. *Soliman*, the Court held that the IRS will weigh the relative importance of the business activities conducted at home against those that are done outside the home.

In *Soliman*, the taxpayer was an anesthesiologist who practiced in three Washington, D.C.-area hospitals, none of which provided him with office space. He therefore established an office in a spare room in his house, in which he maintained patient files, journals, billing records and the like.

In an eight-to-one decision, Justice Kennedy, writing for the majority, held that the essential question is a comparative one: whether the home office is the place where the taxpayer's most important professional activities are performed based on the importance of the activities and the time devoted to them. The service performed by an anesthesiologist is treating patients in hospitals, not reading records in a home office. The doctor's principal place of business was, therefore, the hospitals, and the home office deduction was disallowed, since the home office was used only for administrative aspects of the doctor's business.

The Court stated that it does not matter whether the home office is legitimate or necessary; rather, the issue is whether it is, in fact, the principal place of business based on the Court's new interpretation of "principal." Justice Kennedy stated that the common sense interpretation of principal requires an evaluation of the places where the taxpayer's work is performed. The one where the taxpayer actually performs the most significant tasks will be considered the "principal" place of business.

What This Means To You

For photographers, the implication of this ruling is troubling. The Supreme Court's decision has far-reaching implications for the photography profession. Consider the situation in which a photographer who may be considered as working on location, as Dr. Soliman was, has a darkroom in her home—would that change the facts of *Commissioner* v. *Soliman* sufficiently to allow for a home deduction? The answer is unclear. It is, therefore, prudent for you to consult with your tax adviser before establishing, maintaining, or attempting to take a deduction for a home office.

Is the Office-at-Home Deduction Worthwhile?

If a photographer meets one of the tests outlined above, the next question is what tax benefits can result. The answer, after close analysis, is frequently, "not very many." An *allocable portion* of mortgage interest and property taxes can be deducted against the business. These would be deductible anyway as itemized deductions. The advantage of deducting them against the business is that this reduces the business profit that is subject to self-employment taxes.

Of course, a taxpayer who lives in a rented house and otherwise qualifies for the office-at-home deductions may deduct a portion of the rent that would not otherwise be tax deductible.

The primary tax advantage comes from a deduction for an allocable portion of repairs, utility bills, and depreciation that otherwise would not be deductible at all.

To arrive at the allocable portion, take the square footage of the space used for the business and divide that by the total square footage of the house. Multiply this fraction by your mortgage interest, property taxes, etc., for the amount to be deducted. How to determine the amount of allowable depreciation is too complex to discuss here, and you should discuss this with your accountant or tax advisor.

The total amount that can be deducted for an office or storage place in the home is artificially limited. To determine the amount that can be deducted, take the total amount of money earned in the business and subtract the allocable portion of mortgage interest and property taxes, and the other deductions allocable to the business. The remainder is the maximum amount that you can deduct for the allocable portion of repairs, utilities, and depreciation. In other words, your total business deductions in this situation cannot be greater than your total business income minus all other business expenses. The home-office deduction, therefore, cannot be used to create a net loss. But disallowed losses can be carried forward and deducted in future years.

Besides the obvious complexity of the rules and the mathematics, there are several other factors that limit the benefit of taking a deduction for a studio or office in the home. One of these is the partial loss of the *nonrecognition of gain* (tax-deferred) treatment that is otherwise allowed when a taxpayer sells a principal residence. Ordinarily, when someone sells a principal residence for profit, the tax on the gain is deferred if the seller purchases another principal residence of at least the same value within two years. Most of the tax on this gain is never paid during the taxpayer's lifetime.

This deferral of gain, however, is not allowed to the extent that the house was used in the business.

For example, if you have been claiming twenty percent of your home as a business deduction, when you sell the home you will enjoy a tax deferral on only eighty percent of the profit. The other twenty percent will be subject to tax because that twenty percent represents the sale of a business asset.

In essence, for the price of a current deduction you may be converting what is essentially a nonrecognition, or tax-deferred, asset into a trade or business property.

However, there is one important exception that can work to your advantage. The IRS has ruled that *if you stop qualifying* for the office-at-home tax deduction for at least one year before you sell the house, you are entitled to the entire gain as *rollover*, no matter how many years you have been taking the deduction. (A rollover means you can reinvest the proceeds of the sale in another dwelling within the prescribed period and avoid paying taxes.)

The word *qualifying* in the IRS ruling has a very technical meaning. It does not only mean that you stop taking the business deduction for one year. It also means that you physically move the business out of your home so that it no longer qualifies as an office at home, whether or not you have taken it as a tax deduction. The same ruling applies to the one-time tax exemption of up to $125,000 on the sale of a home by persons over age fifty-five. If you plan to sell any time soon, check all this out with an accountant or tax advisor. A little planning might save you a great deal of money.

Alerting the IRS

Another concern is that by deducting for an office in the home, the taxpayer in effect puts a red flag on the tax return. Obviously, when the tax return expressly asks whether expenses are being deducted for an office in the home, the question is not being asked for purely academic reasons. Although only the IRS knows how much the answer to this question affects someone's chances of being audited, there is no doubt that a "yes" answer does increase the likelihood of an audit.

Given this increased possibility of audit, it doesn't pay to deduct for an office in the home in doubtful situations. Taxpayers who lose the deduction must pay back taxes plus interest or fight in court. One unfortunate taxpayer not only lost the deduction on a technicality, but also lost the rollover treatment on the sale of his home.

If you believe that your studio, dark room, or office at home could qualify for the business deduction, you would be well advised to consult with a competent tax expert who can assist in calculating the deduction.

WHAT TO KNOW
ABOUT LEASES
AND INSURANCE

Photographers may work out of their home, buy the office building they use, or rent their commercial space. The home office deduction has been discussed elsewhere in this text. Purchasing commercial real estate is quite complex and beyond the scope of this book—before embarking on this course, you should retain an experienced real estate lawyer for assistance. In this chapter, we will consider leases and the very important subject of insurance. This latter subject is very closely regulated by state commissioners and, thus, our discussion will, of necessity, be general. For specific information about insurance, you should contact your state Insurance Commissioner and retain an experienced attorney.

Leases

At some time in your professional life as a photographer, you will be in a position where you may have to evaluate the terms and conditions of a commercial lease. You may also have to examine a residential lease, although these are customarily more tightly regulated by state law than are commercial leases. The relationship between a landlord and a tenant varies from state to state and it is important for you to consult with a local attorney who has some expertise in dealing with this body of law before signing a lease. As a photographer, however, you may wish to call your attorney's attention to some specific items in a commercial lease which could be of great concern to you.

What the Property and Cost Really Involve

One of the most important terms in any lease is the description of the property to be rented. Be sure that the document specifies, in some detail, the area that you are entitled to occupy. If you will be renting a studio in a building with common areas, you should have the responsibilities for those common areas spelled out. Will you be responsible for cleaning and maintaining them, or will the landlord? When will the common areas be open or closed? What other facilities are available to you, such as restrooms, storage, and the like?

Another important item is the cost of the leased space. Will you be paying a flat monthly rental or one which will change based on your earnings at the location? In order to evaluate the cost of the space, you should compare it with other similar spaces in the same locale. Do not be afraid to negotiate for more favorable terms.

Care should be taken to not sign a lease that will restrict you from opening another facility close to the one being rented. In addition, find out if there is an escalator clause which will automatically increase your rent based on some external standard such as the Consumer Price Index, fuel prices, or the like.

If the space you are renting is in a mall which has an "anchor" tenant such as a photography supply store, you should determine whether your proximity to that business is important to your business. If so, you should negotiate for a provision which enables you to terminate your lease if the anchor tenant leaves and is not replaced by a comparable business.

Length of the Lease

It is also important to consider the period of the lease. If you intend to rent a studio for a year or two, it is a good idea to try to get an option to extend. It is likely you will want to advertise and promote your business, and if you move on an annual basis, customers may feel that you are unstable. In addition, occasional customers who return on an irregular basis may not know where to find you after the lease period ends. Besides, moving can result in real headaches in regard to mail.

Long-term leases are recordable in some states. Recording where permitted is generally accomplished by having the lease filed in the same office where a deed to the property would be filed. If you are in a position to record your lease, it is probably a good idea to do so since you will be entitled to receive legal and other notices related to the property. Check with a local real estate title company or real estate attorney for the particulars in your state.

If you enter into a long-term lease, you should attempt to obtain the right to assign or sublet the space, so that you are not locked in if your situation should change. Landlords often impose restrictions on these rights which range from preapproving the assignee or sub-tenant to paying the landlord a fee for exercising the right.

Restrictions To Watch Out For

It is essential for you to determine whether there are any restrictions on the particular activity you wish to perform at the leased premises. For example, the area may be zoned so that you are prohibited from discharging developing chemicals into the sewer system. It is a good idea to insist on a provision which puts the burden of obtaining any permit or variances on the landlord or, if you are responsible for them, allowing you to terminate the lease without penalty if you cannot get the permits or variances.

Be sure that the lease permits you to display any sign or advertising used in connection with your business. It is not uncommon, for example, for historic landmark laws to regulate signs put on old buildings. Can you put a sign in your window or in front of your building? Some zoning laws prohibit this.

Be sure that the real estate is properly zoned since most municipalities prohibit residential use of commercial real estate and vice versa. This subject is discussed in more detail later in this chapter.

Remodeling and Utilities

Photographers should also be aware that extensive remodeling may be necessary for certain spaces to become useful studios. If this is the case, it is important for you to determine who will be responsible for the costs of remodeling. In addition, it is essential to find out whether it will be necessary for you to restore the premises to their original condition when the lease ends. This can be extraordinarily expensive and, in some instances, impossible to accomplish.

If you need special hookups, such as water or electrical lines, find out whether the landlord will provide them or whether you have to bear the cost of having them brought in. Of course, if the leased premises already have the necessary facilities, question the landlord regarding the cost of these utilities. Are they included in the rent or are they to be paid separately?

In some locations, garbage pickup is not a problem, since it is one of the services provided by the municipality. On the other hand, it is common for renters to be responsible for their own trash disposal. In commercial spaces, this can be quite expensive and should be addressed in the lease.

Insurance, Security, and Deliveries

Customarily the landlord will be responsible for the exterior of the building. It will be the landlord's obligation to make sure that it does not leak during rainstorms and that it is properly ventilated. Nevertheless, it is important that the lease deal with the question of responsibility if, for example, the building is damaged and some of your photographs are injured or destroyed. Will you have to take out insurance for the building as well as its contents or will the landlord assume responsibility for building insurance? Similarly, find out whether you will have to obtain liability insurance for injuries that are caused in portions of the building not under your control, such as common hallways and the like. In any case, you should of course have your own liability policy for accidental injuries or accidents that occur on your premises.

You may also wish to consider business interruption insurance to cover your losses when, for example, your business is shut down by a natural disaster, such as a hurricane or tornado.

The best insurance agent with which to deal is one that already has clients who are in business for themselves. That agent is more likely to be able to predict and incorporate your particular needs into your policy. If you are unable to locate such a qualified agent in your area, try consulting with one of the professional organizations, such as the American Society of Media Photographers (ASMP), in Princeton Junction, N.J.; or the Professional Photographers of America (PPA), in Atlanta. These organizations should be able to give you information on local organizations in your area, and provide you with the specific referrals.

A good lease will also contain a provision dealing with security. If you are renting an internal space in a shopping center, it is likely that the landlord will be responsible for external security; this is not universally the case, though, so you should find out about security. If you are renting an entire building, it is customarily your responsibility to provide whatever security you deem important. Does the lease permit you to install locks or alarm systems? If this is something you are going to be interested in, you should get an answer to that question.

Many photographers have materials delivered to their studio at off hours so as to avoid disturbing potential customers. Does the lease have any restrictions regarding time or location of deliveries? If you are dealing with large bulky items and are accepting deliveries or making them, put a provision in your lease that will give you the flexibility you desire.

Zoning: Can You Work and Live There?

If the place you wish to rent will be used as both your personal dwelling and studio, some special problems may arise. It is quite common for zoning laws to prohibit certain forms of commercial activities in dwellings when the area is zoned residential.

Some states have enacted legislation which permits individuals to live in certain industrially-zoned buildings, such as warehouses and the like. This type of legislation began in New York City's Soho district in the late 1960s and has spread throughout the country. Some states permit limited commercial activity to occur in residentially-zoned areas. These activities are customarily restricted to light manufacturing, such as photographers' and artists' studios and professional services, such as lawyers, doctors, and accountants. Rarely will these zoning exceptions permit ongoing retail activities. You should consult with your attorney before attempting to operate out of your home or living in your commercial space.

Get It in Writing

Finally, it is essential to be sure that every item agreed upon between you and the landlord is reduced to writing. This is particularly important when dealing with leases, since many state laws provide that a long-term lease is an interest in land and can only be enforced if it is in writing.

137

The writing may consist of several documents; for example, some malls use a "master lease," which governs the rights and responsibilities of all tenants, plus an individual lease which will deal only with the issues unique to your space. Landlords may also adopt rules and regulations which are binding on all tenants, in addition to leases.

The relationship between landlords and tenants is an ancient one which is undergoing a good deal of change. Care should be taken when examining a location to determine exactly what you can do on the premises and whether the landlord or municipal rules will allow you to use the location for your specific purpose.

Insurance

As a photographer, you probably will need several types of insurance. While it is theoretically possible to insure virtually everything, in fact, as a practical matter, there are some risks which are not worth insuring. In this section, I have discussed some of the more common forms of insurance and identified issues which should be considered when obtaining insurance. Again, to ensure adequate protection, it is best to seek the advice of a qualified insurance agent or broker.

If you are going to purchase any insurance, purchase all of it at the same time and at the same place, if possible. With one broad policy, it is more likely you will be able to include the many more unusual risks associated with the photography business, and at a lower rate, than to try and have several separate policies.

Seeking a policy with a higher than average deductible may save you a considerable amount on your premium, as it eliminates the costs associated with small claims for the insurance company. Also, you should attempt to obtain coverage of up to one million dollars with unlimited risk, as in a "general liability" policy.

A general liability provision covers you for claims of injury to others resulting from your negligence. Coverage includes bodily injury at or away from the studio. If you do fashion work and have models in your studio on a regular basis, it is important that you carry enough liability insurance to cover them in the event they are injured and become unable to work. You should check your automobile coverage to see if it covers models if they become injured while you transport them to and from work. Liability coverage can be extended to include legal injury, such as invasion of privacy, copyright violations, and libel.

Another consideration in determining how much coverage you need would be to factor in those risks that could potentially wipe out your business as well as personal assets, such as third person liability or a disabling injury to yourself.

Find out what the labor laws are regarding employee status and workmen's compensation. As a photographer, it is likely you may employ models, assistants, and the like on a temporary or part-time permanent basis; and you may be required to provide income for these employees who are unable to work due to illness or injury. Also, if you have a large permanent staff, you may want to consider medical and retirement benefits for your employees.

Individuals applying for medical insurance are generally charged extremely high rates. If you join an organization like the American Society of Media Photographers, you may be able to take advantage of group rates available to members.

To protect your studio and darkroom, look into a package policy that insures against fire, theft, and other hazards. The policy should be carefully worded to include all locations. For your equipment, a camera floater, which is written to cover loss or damage to equipment, is a necessity. The camera floater is usually attached to the package policy. The camera floater can include worldwide coverage for loss and damage to all parts of your equipment. Floaters only cover the equipment specifically listed, so be sure to periodically update your policy. Also, it is common for most floater policies to cover the amount of your cost, less depreciation; therefore, consider getting a "stated value" floater, which reimburses for the current replacement cost.

In addition, you might consider professional malpractice coverage, which would cover any liability you would incur in a situation where your client sued you because her pictures did not turn out as anticipated. For instance, if you leave the lens cover on the camera while shooting a wedding, malpractice insurance will enable you to compensate your customer and will protect you from what might be a disastrous financial liability.

Also available is bailee coverage, which you might consider if you often photograph the property of others and it remains under your control for a period of time. If you are photographing priceless art objects, one of which becomes broken or lost, bailee coverage could be a godsend.

Because a photographer's insurance needs tend to be complicated and tend to vary with the type of photography done, do try to find an insurance broker experienced in serving photographers before signing onto any policy. The ASMP insurance brokers, Taylor & Taylor Associates, Inc., offer a comprehensive insurance package specifically designed for photographers. The package includes separate policies covering most of the insurance needs discussed in this chapter. For more information, contact Taylor and Taylor Associates, Inc., 205 E. 42nd St., New York, N.Y. 10017 (212) 490-8511, 1-800-922-1184.

BASIC TYPES
OF CONTRACTS
AND REMEDIES

In the normal course of business, photographers enter into contracts with magazines, agents, other photographers, customers, or film developers. The contractual terms may vary with the kind of service or image contracted for, but in every case the nature of legally binding agreements is the same.

The word contract commonly brings to mind a long, complicated document replete with legal jargon designed to provide hours of work for lawyers. But this need not be the case. A simple, straightforward contract can be just as valid and enforceable as a complicated one.

What is a Contract?

A contract is defined as a legally binding promise or set of promises. The law requires the participants in a contract to perform the promises they have made to each other. In the event of non-performance—usually called a breach—the law provides remedies to the injured party. For the purposes of this discussion, we will assume that the contract is between two people.

The three basic elements of every contract are the offer, the acceptance, and the consideration. Suppose, for example, you show a potential customer a variety of black-and-white family portraits taken in your studio and suggest what you think would be the best arrangement for photographing her family (the offer). The customer says she likes the way you have photographed other families and wants you to do it the same way for her (the acceptance). You agree on a price (the consideration).

That's the basic framework, but a great many variations can be played on that theme.

Types of Contracts

Contracts may be express or implied; they may be oral or written. On this latter point, there are at least two types of contracts that must be in writing if they are to be legally enforceable: (1) any contract which, by its terms, cannot be completed in less than one year; and (2) any contract that involves the sale of goods for over $500.

An express contract is one in which all the details are spelled out. Suppose, for example, you make a contract with a sculptor to deliver fifty slides of his work, to be delivered on or before October 1, at an agreed-upon price, which will be paid thirty days after the slides are delivered.

That's fairly straightforward. If either party fails to live up to any material part of the contract, a breach has occurred, and the other party may withhold performance of his or her obligation until receiving assurance that the breaching party will perform. In the event no such assurance is forthcoming, the aggrieved party may have reason to take action and go to court for breach of contract.

If the slides are delivered on October 15 and the sculptor had needed to get them to the judges for a juried exhibit by October 10, time was an important consideration and the sculptor would not be required to accept the late delivery. But if time is not a material consideration, then the tardy delivery would probably be considered "substantial performance" and the sculptor would have to accept the delivery in spite of the delay. Note, a small minority of jurisdictions would require strict performance despite the fact that the contract did not provide that time was of the essence. In these states, the sculptor may consider a late delivery to be a breach.

Express contracts can be either oral or written, though if you are going to the trouble of expressing contractual terms, you should put your understanding in writing.

Implied contracts need not be very complicated either, though they are usually not done in writing. Suppose you call a printer to order 1,000 sheets of letterhead without making an express statement that you will pay for the printing. The promise to pay is implied in the order, and is enforceable when the stationery is picked up.

But with implied contracts, things can often become a lot stickier. Suppose an acquaintance asks you, a well-known wildlife photographer, to bring over one of your recent large prints of a nesting eagle to see how it will look in her living room. She asks if you would leave it there for a few days. Two months later she still has it, and you overhear her raving to others about how marvelous it looks over the fireplace.

Is there an implied contract to purchase in this arrangement? That may depend on whether you are normally in the business of selling your work, or whether you usually loan your work for approval.

Most contracts that photographers enter into in terms of their work involve some aspect of the sale of that work.

Another kind of implied contract will arise when somebody requests you to send them your work. When, for example, Nike Corporation requested sports-action photographer, Don Johnson, to send his portfolio to the corporation, there was an implied agreement that Nike would take reasonable care of the portfolio and return it in due course. When the portfolio was lost at Nike, Johnson sued and recovered for his lost work.

Let's examine the principles of offer, acceptance, and consideration in the context of several potential situations for a hypothetical freelance photographer, Pat Smith.

Smith has had works accepted in local and regional exhibitions, has won several prizes, and is getting assignments from large national corporations. In a word, Smith is developing quite a reputation. With this brief background, we'll look at the following situations and see whether an enforceable contract comes into existence.

- At a cocktail party, Jones expresses an interest in hiring Smith to photograph Jones's family. "It looks like your work will go up in price pretty soon," Jones tells Smith. "I'm going to hire you while I can still afford you."

Is this a contract? If so, what are the terms of the offer—the particular work, the specific price? No, this is not really an offer that Smith can accept. It is nothing more than an opinion or a vague expression of intent.

- Brown offers to pay $400 for one of Smith's photographs that she saw in a show several months ago. At the show it was listed at $450, but Smith agrees to accept the lower price.

Is this an enforceable contract? Yes! Brown has offered, in unambiguous terms, to pay a specific amount for a specific work, and Smith has accepted the offer. A binding contract exists.

- One day Gray shows up at Smith's studio and sees a photograph which she would like to use in her book. She offers $200 for the exclusive publication rights in the photograph. Smith accepts and promises to deliver the photograph to Gray's publisher next week, at which time Gray will pay for the rights. An hour later, Brown shows up. She likes the same photograph and offers Smith $300 for the exclusive publishing rights in it. Can Smith accept the later offer?

No—a contract exists with Gray. An offer was made and accepted. The fact that the rights have not yet been exercised or paid for does not make the contract any less binding.

- Green agrees that Smith will photograph Green's wedding and present Green with an acceptable wedding album for $1,000. It is understood that Smith will take a variety of shots throughout the festivities. After Smith presents Green with the proofs, Green indicates that he is disappointed and will not accept any of them.

Green is making the offer in this case, but the offer is conditional upon his satisfaction with the completed work. Smith can only accept the offer by producing something that meets Green's subjective standards—a risky business. There is no enforceable contract for payment until such time as Green indicates that the completed album is satisfactory.

Suppose Green came to Smith's studio and said that the completed album was satisfactory but then, when Smith delivers it, says it doesn't look right when Green reexamines it at home. That's too late for Green to change his mind. The contract became binding at the moment he indicated that the album was satisfactory. If he then refuses to accept it, he would be breaching his contract.

Earlier I mentioned that contracts for goods worth over $500 must be in writing. Under the Uniform Commercial Code, which governs contracts for the sale of goods (see page 161), a commission to produce a work is a personal-service contract, as distinct from a contract for the sale of a piece already completed. Therefore, the UCC does not generally apply to commissions. (Bill of Sale and Commission Agreement Forms are included at the end of this chapter.)

It is not clear whether the hypothetical situation described above would be considered a contract for the sale of future goods—a wedding album that will be delivered—or whether the agreement would be considered a contract for services the wedding photographer is performing. There is at least one case which suggests that these facts would give rise to a contract for the sale of future goods and be within the coverage of the UCC.

Oral or Written Contracts?

Contracts are enforceable only if they can be proven. The hypothetical examples mentioned above could have been oral contracts, but a great deal of detail is often lost in the course of remembering a conversation. The best practice, of course, is to get it in writing. A written contract not only provides proof, but makes very clear the understanding of both parties regarding the agreement and its terms.

Some people are adamant about doing business strictly on a handshake, particularly where photography is concerned. The assumption seems to be that the best business relations are those based upon mutual trust. And some business people believe that any agreement other than a gentlemen's agreement belies this trust.

Although there may be some validity to these assumptions, people who own small businesses, such as photographers, would nevertheless be well advised to put all of their oral agreements into writing. Far too many people have suffered adverse consequences because of their reliance upon the sanctity of oral contracts.

Even in the best of business relationships, it is still possible that one or both parties might forget the terms of an oral agreement. Or both parties might have quite different perceptions about the precise terms of the agreement reached. When, however, the agreement is put into writing, there is much less doubt as to the terms of the arrangement. Thus a written contract generally functions as a safeguard against subsequent misunderstanding or forgetful minds. In addition, a written contract avoids what is perhaps the principal problem with oral contracts: the fact that they cannot always be proven or enforced.

When Written Contracts Are Necessary

Even if there is no question that an oral contract was made, it may not always be enforceable. There are some agreements which the law requires to be in writing.

An early law that was designed to prevent fraud and perjury, known as the Statute of Frauds, provides that any contract which by its terms cannot be fully performed within one year must be in writing. This rule is narrowly interpreted, so if there is any possibility, no matter how remote, that the contract could be fully performed within one year, the contract need not be reduced to writing.

Assume that a customer and a photographer have entered into a contract in which the photographer has agreed to produce five pictures. Assume further that the agreement requires that the photographer submit one set of proofs per year for five years. In this situation, the terms of the agreement make it impossible for the photographer to complete

145

performance within one year. If, however, the photographer agrees to submit five sets of proofs within a five-year period, it is possible that the photographer could submit all five sets in the first year; therefore, the Statute of Frauds would not apply and the agreement need not be in writing to be enforceable. The fact that the photographer might not actually complete performance within one year is immaterial. So long as complete performance within one year is possible, the agreement may be oral.

The Statute of Frauds further provides that certain agreements relating to the sale of goods must be in writing to be enforceable. This provision was codified in the Uniform Sales Act and has now been incorporated into the Uniform Commercial Code. The UCC provides that a contract for the sale of goods costing over $500 is not enforceable unless it is in writing and is signed by the party against whom enforcement is sought. There is no such monetary restriction on service contracts, however. Regardless of the amount of payment, a contract for the sale of services which can be completed within one year need not be in writing.

Distinguishing Sale of Goods from Sale of Services

Obviously, it is important to know whether a particular contract is regarded as involving the sale of goods or the sale of services. The UCC defines goods as being all things that are movable at the time the contract is made, with the exception of the money (or investment securities or certain other types of documents) used as payment for the goods. This definition is sufficiently broad to enable most courts to find that the transactions between a photographer and a supplier of such items as film, paper, cameras, and tripods involve goods. Unfortunately, the distinction is not so clear in the case of agreements between a photographer and a customer.

At least one court has ruled that the photographer-customer contract is a contract for the sale of goods, i.e., completed works. In this case, a contract to take wedding pictures was held to be a contract for the sale of goods and thus enforceable.

Determining the Contract Price of Goods

Assuming for the moment that the various agreements entered into by the photographer involve a sale of goods, a second matter to be determined is whether the price of the goods exceeds $500. In most cases, the answer will be clear—but not always.

A photographer, for example, might contract to purchase several camera accessories from a wholesaler. The price for the total purchase exceeds $500, but the price for the individual accessories does not. Which price determines whether or not the statute applies?

Or suppose a photographer sells pictures to a gallery. The gallery will offer the pictures at a price that exceeds $500, but the price the photographer gets is less than $500. Again, which price is used to determine whether the statute applies?

The UCC and the cases interpreting this law provide some guidelines for determining the contract price of goods. The statute provides that the definition of price is to be broadly interpreted to include a payment in money or some other thing of value. The definition of goods in the UCC may be sufficiently broad to include the camera accessories but the problem of the sale of pictures to the gallery remains.

Obviously, a photographer will not in every case be able to ascertain whether the financial terms of a given contract exceed $500, any more than one can always be certain whether a given agreement involves the sale of goods or of services. Given the differences in interpretation by various courts, the best way to ensure that a contract will be enforceable is to put it in clear, unambiguous writing.

No-Cost Written Agreements

At this point, a photographer might claim, with reason, that his or her profession is taking photographs, not writing legal documents. Where is he or she going to find the extra time, energy, or patience to draft contracts?

Fortunately, you as a photographer will not always need to do this, since the supplier or customers you deal with may be willing to draft satisfactory contracts. However, be wary of someone else's all-purpose contracts—they will almost invariably be one-sided, with all terms drafted in favor of whoever paid to have them prepared.

As a second alternative, you could employ an attorney to draft your contracts. But this may be worthwhile only where the contract involves a substantial transaction. With smaller transactions, the legal fees may be larger than any benefits you'd receive.

It is worth noting that the book entitled *Business and Legal Forms for Photographers*, published by Allworth Press, is an excellent resource and contains many useful forms and documents.

The Uniform Commercial Code, a compilation of commercial laws enacted in every state except Louisiana, provides a third and perhaps the best alternative. You need not draft a contract at all or rely on a supplier, customer, or attorney to do so.

The UCC provides that where both parties are merchants and one party sends to the other a written confirmation of an oral contract within a reasonable time after that contract was made, and the recipient does not object to the confirming memorandum within ten days of its receipt, the contract will be deemed enforceable.

A merchant is defined as any person who normally deals in goods of the kind sold or who by occupation represents himself as having knowledge or skill peculiar to the practices or goods involved in the transaction. Thus professional photographers and their suppliers will be deemed merchants. Even an amateur photographer will be considered a merchant, since adopting the designation "photographer" would be deemed as representing oneself as having special knowledge or skill in the field. The rule will therefore apply to many oral contracts you might make. Consumers, such as individuals who wish to have a family portrait taken, are probably not merchants within the meaning of the statute.

It should be emphasized that the sole effect of the confirming memorandum is that neither party can use the Statute of Frauds as a defense, assuming that the recipient fails to object within ten days after receipt. The party sending the confirming memorandum must still prove that an oral contract was, in fact, made prior to or at the same time as the written confirmation. But once such proof is offered, neither party can raise the Statute of Frauds to avoid enforcement of agreement.

The advantage of the confirming memorandum over a written contract is that the confirming memorandum can be used without the active participation of the other contracting party. It would suffice, for example, to simply state: This memorandum is to confirm our oral agreement.

But since the writer would still have to prove the terms of that agreement, it would be useful to provide a bit more detail in the confirming memorandum, such as the subject of the contract, the date it was made, and the price or other consideration to be paid. Thus you might draft something like the following:

> This memorandum is to confirm our oral agreement made on July 3, 1995, pursuant to which (photographer) agreed to deliver to (magazine editor) on or before September 19, 1995, five photographs and the right to use each of them one time only in your October issue for the price of $200.

The advantages of providing some detail to the confirming memorandum are twofold. First, in the event of a dispute, the photographer could introduce the memorandum as proof of the terms of the oral agreement. And second, the recipient of the memorandum will be precluded from offering any proof regarding the terms of the oral contract that contradicts the terms contained in the memorandum. The recipient or, for that matter, the party sending the memorandum, can only introduce proof regarding the terms of the oral contract that are consistent with the terms found in the memorandum. Thus, the editor in the above example would be precluded from claiming that the contract called for delivery of six photographs because the quantity was stated in the memo and not objected to.

On the other hand, the editor would be permitted to testify that the original contract required the photographer to package the pictures in a specific way since this testimony would not contradict the terms stated in the memorandum.

One party to a contract can prevent the other from adding or inventing terms not covered in the confirming memorandum by ending the memo with a clause requiring all other provisions to be contained in a written and signed document. Such a clause might read:

> This is the entire agreement between the parties and no modification, alteration, or additional terms shall be enforceable unless in writing and signed by both parties.

To sum up, no one in business should rely on oral contracts alone since they offer little protection in the event of a dispute. The best protection is afforded by a written contract. It is a truism that oral contracts are not worth the paper on which they are written. Where a complete written contract is too burdensome or too costly, the photographer should at least submit a memorandum in confirmation of an oral contract. That at least surpasses the initial barrier raised by the Statute of Frauds. Moreover, by recounting the terms in the memorandum, you, the photographer, will be in a much better position later on to prove the oral contract.

Summary of Essentials to Put in Writing

A contract rarely need be—or should be—a long, complicated document written in legal jargon designed to provide a handsome income to lawyers. Indeed, a contract should be written in simple language that both parties can understand, and should spell out the terms of the agreement.

The contract should include: (1) the date of the agreement; (2) identification of the two parties; (3) a description of the work being sold or, if a service, the service to be performed; (4) the price; and (5) the signatures of the two parties.

To supplement these basics, the agreement should spell out whatever other terms might be applicable: pricing arrangements, payment schedules, copyright ownership, use rights, licenses, etc.

Finally, it should be noted that a written document that leaves out essential terms presents many of the same problems of proof and ambiguity as an oral contract. Contract terms should be well conceived, clearly drafted, "conspicuous" (i.e., not in tiny print that no one can read), and in plain English so everyone understands what the terms are.

Questionable and Broken Contracts

Obviously, you do not want to find yourself involved in contracts of questionable validity, nor do you want to find yourself stuck with a contract that has not been honored. In the first case, how do you spot them; in the second case, what can you do to get justice?

Capacity to Contract

Certain classes of people are deemed by law to lack capacity to contract. The most obvious class is minors, a fact of particular relevance to photographers since a photographer might wish to use a minor as a model. A person is legally a minor until the age of majority, which varies from state to state, but in most cases is either eighteen or twenty-one. A contract entered into by a minor is not necessarily void, but generally is voidable. This means that the minor is free to rescind the contract until reaching the age of majority, but that the other party is bound by the contract if the minor elects to enforce it. In some states a minor over eighteen must restore the consideration (payment) or its equivalent as a condition of rescission. Some states allow a parent to sign on behalf of a minor (see model release forms at the end of chapter 3); other states have a procedure for enabling minors to sign binding nonrescindable contracts. This generally requires the approval of a judge. Other people who lack the capacity to contract include insane and incompetent persons. Since the requirements for contracting with such persons are highly technical, the photographer who wishes to do so would be well advised to consult a lawyer.

Illegal Contracts

If either the consideration (which is normally money) or the subject matter of the contract is illegal, the contract itself is illegal. This problem will not normally arise in photography contracts, but it is possible that a photographer could unwittingly become a party to an illegal contract. For example, the state of New York has enacted a statute, popularly known as the Son of Sam Law, that prohibits criminals from receiving financial compensation from the exploitation and commercialization of their crimes. Such statutes are being increasingly adopted. Presently, the federal government and the vast majority of states have

Son of Sam laws. A publisher who contracts to pay a criminal royalties in return for the criminal's story would be violating the statute, and the contract would therefore be illegal. The same would probably be true of an agreement made by a photographer to illustrate a criminal's story in exchange for some payment. It is not certain, however, whether someone could circumvent the statute by paying a criminal for other services. *Life* magazine paid $9,000 to Bernard Welch, convicted murderer of Michael Halberstam, for the exclusive rights to photographs from the Welch family album. It remains to be seen whether such pictures would fall within the scope of a Son of Sam type of statute.

A photographer may also become a party to an illegal contract if the work resulting from that contract is found to be either obscene or libelous. (Obscenity is discussed in chapter 4 and libel, in chapter 2.)

Generally, a photographer is not liable for a deceptive or fraudulent use of his work unless he knew his work would be used in a dishonest manner, in which event the contract would be deemed void and liability also may result. Even so, a photographer should always try to guard against potential fraud claims by avoiding participation in a deception. As a general rule, if the subject matter to be photographed is obviously misleading, beware.

The Federal Trade Commission is responsible for preventing "unfair methods of competition in commerce and unfair or deceptive acts or practices in commerce." This act also explicitly makes persons, partnerships, and corporations liable for deceptive advertising. The FTC has the authority to issue orders requiring corrective advertising.

There is no hard and fast rule for determining what constitutes an unfair or deceptive act or practice. As for deceptive advertising, the phrase means an advertisement that is materially misleading. An advertisement is deceptive if it has the "tendency" or "capacity" to deceive the public. The Commission may examine an advertisement and determine its potential effect on the minds of consumers without considering public opinion or even hearing evidence by complaining parties. The Commission may even find an advertisement violates the FTC Act despite consumers' testimony that they would not be misled by it. For instance, the truth in advertising law provides that a photographer will be liable for any deception in shooting an advertisement. General Foods issued a policy statement regarding food photography which provides useful guidelines for any photographer.

- Food will be photographed in an unadulterated state—the product must be typical of that normally packed; with no preselection for quality or substitution of individual components.
- Individual portions must conform to amount per serving used in describing yield.
- Package amounts shown must conform to package yield.

- The product must be prepared according to package directions.
- A recipe must follow directions and be shown in the same condition it would appear in when suitable for serving.
- Mock-ups may not be used.
- Props should be typical of those readily available to the consumers.
- Theatrical devices (unusual camera angles, small-size bowls and spoons) may not be used to make false implications.

The law generally treats an illegal contract as void rather than merely voidable—an important distinction. A voidable contract is valid until it is voided by the party possessing the right to rescind, whereas a void contract is not binding on either party, and neither party will be permitted to enjoy any fruits of the agreement. A void contract results when both parties are at fault or where the illegality involves a morally reprehensible crime. If, however, the illegality involves an act which is wrong only because the law says that it is (as, for example, illegal parking or not obtaining a necessary business license), one party may have some rights against the less innocent party. A photographer who anticipates entering into, or is already involved in, a contract of questionable legality would be well advised to consult a lawyer.

Unconscionable Contracts

The law generally gives the parties involved in a contract complete freedom to contract. Thus, contractual terms which are unfair, unjust, or even ludicrous will generally be enforced if they are legal. But this freedom is not without limits; the parties are not free to make a contract which is unconscionable. Unconscionability is an elusive concept, but the courts have certain guidelines in ruling on it. A given contract is likely to be considered unconscionable if it is grossly unfair and the parties lack equal bargaining power. Photographers who are just starting out are typically in a weaker bargaining position than advertising clients or owners of stock photo businesses and are therefore more likely to win a suit on an allegation of unconscionability. This is especially true where the photographer has simply signed a magazine's form contract. If the form contract is extremely one-sided in favor of the magazine, and if the photographer was given the choice of signing the contract unchanged or not contracting at all, a court could find that the agreement was unconscionable. If that happens, the court may either treat the contract as void or strike the unconscionable clauses and enforce the remainder. It should be noted that unconscionability is generally used as a defense by the one who is sued for breach of contract, and that the defense is rarely successful, particularly where both parties are business people.

What Happens When a Contract Is Broken?

The principle underlying all remedies for breach of contract is to satisfy the wronged party's expectations: that is, the courts will attempt to place the injured party in the position that would have resulted had the contract been fully performed. Courts and the legislatures have devised a number of remedies to provide aggrieved parties with the benefit of their bargains. Generally, this will take the form of monetary damages, but where monetary damages fail to solve the problem, the court may order *specific performance*. Specific performance means the breaching party is ordered to perform as promised. This remedy is generally reserved for cases in which the contract involves unique goods. In photography, a court might specifically enforce a contract to produce wedding pictures by compelling the photographer to deliver the photographs to the customer, but only if the photographs had been printed, qualifying as goods. A court would not be likely to compel a photographer to shoot or develop prints (thus performing a service) as a means of satisfying the aggrieved customer. The Thirteenth Amendment of the Constitution prohibits one from being forced to perform labor against one's will. Thus, for breach of a personal-service contract, monetary damages are generally awarded.

Photos Kept Too Long

Frequently, photographers or photo agencies will submit prints or transparencies to a potential purchaser on approval. If this submission is the result of an oral agreement, i.e., the photos were requested, the customer may be liable for holding fees if the photographs are kept for an unreasonable time without payment.

Ordinarily, the delivery memos that accompany requested photographs contain clauses specifying that the customer is liable for any loss or damage to the photographs. A delivery memo may contain provisions that specify a certain amount the customer must pay for each lost or damaged picture. These provisions are enforceable if the amount they specify is a reasonable estimate of the value of the photos and not a penalty. Delivery memos are designed to be signed and returned by the customer; however, they are usually effective and enforceable even if not signed.

Damages Against Loss of Film or Photographs

The law allows recovery of damages against film processors who lose or damage film, or, in some cases, who lose or damage photographs.

However, recovery may be limited to the cost of the film alone. In *Goor* v. *Navilio* the plaintiff's vacation pictures were lost by the photo lab to which he entrusted them for processing. The film carton had the following disclaimer: "The film in this carton has been made with great care and will be processed in our laboratory without additional charge. If we find the film to have been defective in manufacture or to have been damaged in our laboratory, we will replace it, but we assume no other responsibility either express or implied." The court held that recovery was limited to the replacement cost of the film because of the written disclaimer.

In *Willard Van Dyke Productions* v. *Eastman Kodak* the facts are similar to those in *Goor* except that the film carton stated that the processing was not included in the price of the film; therefore, the court allowed full recovery of lost profits.

In *Mieske* v. *Bartell Drug Co.* the plaintiff was a home photographer who sued a drugstore for losing the plaintiff's thirty-two reels of home movie film. Although the drugstore gave the plaintiff a receipt that included a clause disclaiming liability beyond the retail cost of the film, the court found the disclaimer invalid and unconscionable. The court reasoned that Article 2 of the Uniform Commercial Code, which provides that unconscionable disclaimers will not be upheld, applies to bailments as well as to the sale of goods. Bailment is the rightful temporary possession of someone else's property; parking a car in a parking lot, for example, establishes a bailment, as does leaving film with a processor. The court noted that such disclaimers should not be upheld between a commercial film processor and a retail customer because retail customers probably do not notice or understand a disclaimer clause on a receipt. However, such a disclaimer might be valid among people within the photography industry—people who would be expected to know about and understand the disclaimer.

You should carefully read any limitation of liability agreement before signing it, since it has been held that these provisions are enforceable. When, for example, a stock photography agency was unable to deliver a photographer's work, litigation resulted.

The photographer, who was also an attorney, admitted that he signed a standard photography agency agreement which stated that the photographer agreed to obtain his own insurance, and that the agency exercising reasonable care, would not be held responsible for the loss or damage to the pictures.

The court held that the limitation of liability agreement was enforceable, at least absent any gross negligence or unconscionability on the part of the agency.

Concerning the amount of recovery, the cases all show that the photographer can always recover at least the cost of the damaged film. In addition, the photographer can often recover the value of the photographs that would have resulted had the film been processed properly.

There are various ways in which courts determine the damages a photographer receives in such cases. As a first step, the court will attempt to calculate the market value of photographs that would have been made from the lost or damaged film. Market value is determined by the prior use made of the photograph, the current price for use of such photographs, and the extent to which the photograph has already been used. For example, an old (though not an antique) transparency or negative might have less value than a newer one because its useful life as a commercial photograph is shorter. On the other hand, it might have historical importance. Also, certain subjects are more commercially valuable or salable than others. Finally, courts consider the ease with which certain pictures may be retaken.

Sometimes the market value of film or pictures is hard to ascertain. In such cases, courts have uniformly held that a variety of factors may be used to determine the value of the film or photographs. One case involved a well-known scientist/photographer who delivered to the Museum of Natural History original color transparencies of indigenous species he took in the Antarctic. The museum failed to return eleven of the transparencies. The photographer attempted to establish the cost of replacement or reproduction of the transparencies, based upon either the actual cash outlay or the value of the required labor and materials. In his testimony, the photographer told the court that the location where the transparencies were taken was remote; the transparencies were taken underwater, which was extremely hazardous; they were the best of the shots he took; and they had "data value," i.e., it was impossible to reproduce the conditions under which the pictures were taken.

The court determined that the fair and reasonable value of the transparencies was $15,000 because if there is a total loss of property with no ascertainable market value, the measure of damages is the cost to replace or reproduce the article and if it cannot be reproduced or replaced, then its actual value to the owner should be considered in fixing damages.

In one case, photographer Brian Wolff realized the importance of having his paperwork in order. When *Geo* magazine had seventy-six of his photos stolen from it, it became necessary to identify each chrome and place a value on it. Fortunately, the photographer's proofs contained this essential information. In another case, one issue was the value of the photographer's lost slides. Experts in the industry testified that fifteen hundred dollars per transparency was reasonable given the photographer's status, the sales price for his other works, and the fact that some of the photos were irreplaceable. Fifteen hundred dollars appears to be the standard price for a lost slide by a professional photographer, yet some works have been valued even higher. For ex-

155

ample, John G. Zimmerman received three thousand dollars per slide in 1988, when he was able to establish the exceptional and irreplaceable nature of his action-oriented slides spanning a forty-year period. Similarly, photographer John Stevens recovered over twenty-two thousand dollars for a lost slide of Salvador Dali.

Photographer Ethan Hoffman won a substantial judgment against Portogallo, Inc., when the lab lost ten rolls of film which were part of a larger series. The court awarded the photographer $1,500 per lost image for a total of $486,000 ($632,586 with interest added) based on the uniqueness of the subject matter, Hoffman's status as a prestigious photojournalist, and the number of times his work had been published. In addition, Hoffman had commitments from two major magazines to publish some of the lost pictures. Unfortunately, the judgment may be uncollectible since the lab promptly ceased doing business.

You may desire to have a "liquidated damages clause" included in your contracts. Such a clause should provide that because of the difficulty in ascertaining actual damages, the parties have agreed on a per-item value, and that the specified value is reasonable. It should also state that the photographer would not sell the rights to any of the items for less than the stated amount.

In 1991, a Texas court upheld such a clause and awarded a photographer $51,000 for the loss of thirty-four of his slides. The court stated that a liquidated damages provision will be enforced if the harm caused is: "(1) incapable or difficult of estimation; and (2) the amount of liquidated damages is a reasonable forecast of just compensation."

The Assignment Agreement

Whenever you contract with a client for an assignment, whether it is a one-time shoot, or a long-term assignment, there is always the possibility that someone will change their mind, or circumstances will change such that you, as the photographer, are left with no assignment, having already, perhaps, incurred some expense in preparation. In order to protect yourself against this happening, it is best to enter into an assignment agreement which details the consequences for either party's breach. (See the end of this chapter for a sample agreement.)

First, be sure to be clear on how you expect to be paid; i.e., whether it is per day or per photograph, as well as time of payment. You should include a clause on travel, preparation, and weather days. It is standard to receive one-half fee for travel and weather cancellations. If you are being paid per day, specify how overtime is to be considered—whether by the week or by the day. This is especially important if you are going to be expected to put in long days. You should also predetermine whose responsibility it is to rent the space you will be using, and who is paying for it. Include the amount of expenses you are anticipating along with an ability to exceed the budget by ten percent without prior approval. This will protect you in the event of unanticipated overages.

The contract should, of course, specify the number and size of photographs requested, as well as a brief description of their content.

A cancellation policy will most likely vary according to the type of assignment. If it is possible to schedule a reshoot in the near future that will not interfere with the result or your schedule, you may decide to waive a cancellation charge providing your client gives you reasonable notice. However, if you do not get notice, try to provide for one-half fees in the agreement, along with an additional one-half fee plus expenses for any reshoot. This is an area that you will most likely need to rely on all of your tact and negotiating skills in dealing with your client.

If you are presented with a contract by your client, read it carefully to determine whether it states that the work is a "work for hire." If so, the copyright in the work will belong to the client, not you. Any assignment contract should explicitly state that the copyright in the work belongs to you, or that rights not granted are reserved to you.

Ownership of the original photographs and negatives also should be discussed—will the client receive the originals and/or negatives, or only permission to reproduce?

You should require your client to obtain any necessary releases and to indemnify you for any costs you incur as a result of the client's not doing so.

Depending on how the photograph is to be used, you may also wish to specify the credit line, if any, to be used.

The Bill of Sale on page 158 and the Commission Agreement on pages 159–60 will be of special value to fine arts photographers. If the photographer wishes to include special terms and conditions on the reverse of the Bill of Sale, the discussion of contracts on pages 145–150 should be referred to. The Assignment Estimate/Confirmation/Invoice form on pages 161–62 is reproduced by permission from *Business and Legal Forms for Photographers* by Tad Crawford.

Bill of Sale

Terms: ☐ Cash Sale   ☐ Bank Americard

Net   ☐ Master Charge   Credit Card #:

Ship to: _____ Bill to: _____   Date

    _____   _____

    _____   _____   Via

Item No.	Description: Medium, Title, Dimensions (Height × Width)	Price

All sales subject to terms and conditions on reverse of this invoice.   Net

Received in good condition:

Sales tax

Client's signature _____

   Date _____   Total

158

Commission Agreement

WHEREAS _____ (Artist), is a creator of art works desiring to create

a(n) _____ [(include appropriate

item) painting, sculpture, drawing, work of graphic art, etching, lithograph, offset print, silkscreen print, seriograph, photograph, or craftwork executed in textile, fiber, wood, plastic, glass or similar materials] (Work), and

WHEREAS _____ (Patron), desires to commission the Work,

NOW THEREFORE, the Artist and the Patron agree to the following provisions:

1. The Artist agrees to create the Work. The Parties agree that the Artist is an independent contractor, not an employee of the Patron; that the Artist is not being paid by the hour but according to the terms of this agreement; and that the Artist's creation of the Work is not a work for hire.
2. The Work will be constructed according to the following specifications:
   a. Size—all dimensions: _____
   b. Materials to be used: _____
   c. Manner of construction: _____
   d. Location of construction: _____
   e. Final location of the Work: _____

3. The Artist agrees to prepare _____ [(include appropriate items and indicate quantity) studies, sketches, models, drawings, maquettes or other examples] for the Patron's approval. Within two weeks of receipt of the [items named above] the Patron may request changes and the Artist will make such changes for an additional fee of $ _____ per hour, provided however, that the Artist shall not be required to work more than _____ hours to make the changes requested.
4. The Work will be completed by _____ [indicate completion date], provided however, under extenuating circumstances that prevent the Artist from working, the Artist may extend the time _____ months.

Alternative Clause 5 for Sculptures
5. The Artist agrees to pay all costs of crating the Work for removal and transportation. The Patron agrees to pay all costs of removing the Sculpture from the Artist's studio, transporting it to the final location, and installing it at the final location. The Artist agrees to submit a site plan and to supervise the installation at the final location. The cost of preparing the site shall be paid by the Patron. The Patron agrees to pay the Artist's transportation and living costs during the installation at the final location.

Alternative Clause 5 for Sculptures
5. The Artist agrees to pay all costs of mounting and framing including the frame, mats, and glass as well as the cost of crating the Work for removal and transportation. The Patron agrees to pay all costs for removing and transporting the Work from the Artist's studio to the final location.

Alternative Clause 5 for Other Works
5. The Artist agrees to pay all costs of crating the Work for removal and transportation. The Patron agrees to pay all costs for removing and transporting the Work from the Artist's studio to the final location.

6. The Artist agrees to provide and pay for all labor, materials, equipment, tools, machinery, water, heat, utilities, transportation and other facilities, and services necessary for the proper completion of the Work.
7. The Artist agrees at all times to enforce strict discipline and good order among employees or subcontractors and agrees not to employ any persons unfit or unskilled in their assigned tasks in connection with completion of the Work.
8. The Artist warrants to the Patron that all materials and equipment incorporated in completing the Work will be new unless otherwise specified and that all work will be of good quality free from known faults and defects.

9. The Patron agrees to pay the Artist as follows:
   a. $ _____ upon signing this Agreement.
   b. $ _____ upon approval by the Patron of the materials prepared by the Artist in accordance with Clause 3 of this Agreement.
   c. $ _____ upon one-half completion of the Work.
   d. $ _____ upon completion of the Work, its final approval and acceptance by the Patron, and prior to its removal from the Artist's studio.
   e. The amounts paid under (a) and (b) above shall not be refundable.

10. The amounts paid by the Patron to the Artist in accordance with Clause 9 include all sales and similar taxes.

11. The Artist agrees to allow the Patron to inspect the Work at her studio during reasonable hours when the Work is one-half complete and again when the Work is completed.

12. The Artist at her expense agrees to keep the Work fully insured until final approval and delivery at the Artist's studio. The Patron agrees at her expense to insure the Work from the time it leaves the Artist's studio until it is installed at the final location.

13. The Patron agrees to purchase and maintain liability insurance and may, at her option, maintain insurance to protect against claims which may arise from operations under this agreement.

14. The Patron agrees to purchase and maintain property insurance upon the completed Work to the full insurable value. This insurance shall include the interests of the Patron, Artist, and subcontractors in the Work and shall insure against the perils of fire and extended coverage, and shall include "all risk" insurance for physical loss or damage including, without duplication of coverage, theft, vandalism and malicious mischief.

15. If the Artist becomes ill, dies, or is otherwise unable to complete the Work by the Completion Date, the Artist agrees to refund to the Patron all amounts paid to the Artist other than the amounts paid in Paragraphs (a) and (b) of Clause 9 of this Agreement. Under such circumstances, with the exception of copyright rights reserved in Clause 19 of this Agreement, the [items named in Clause 3] and the Work (to the extent completed) shall be the property of the Patron.

16. The Artist represents that the Work is unique and that no identical or greatly similar Work will be created by her.

17. Final approval and acceptance of the Work shall be solely within the discretion of the Patron. The Patron agrees to accept or reject the Work by _____ . If the Work is rejected, the amounts paid under Paragraphs (a), (b), and (c) of Clause 9 of this Agreement shall be retained by the Artist, and the Patron shall not be required to pay the amount specified in Paragraph (d) of Clause 9 of this Agreement. If the Work is rejected by the Patron, it and the [items named in Clause 3] shall be the property of the Artist.

18. Patron agrees to consult with the Artist prior to commencement of any repairs or restoration and if practical to employ the Artist if, at any time, the Work becomes damaged.

19. The Parties agree that Copyright of the Work is vested in the Artist.

20. The Artist agrees to affix to the Work a copyright notice sufficient to defeat a defense of innocent infringement, which shall include the copyright symbol, the date and the name of the Artist. The copyright notice shall be attached either to the Work, to the frame or base, or adjacent thereto in a manner so that the notice shall be visible and give reasonable notice of the Artist's copyright ownership.

21. If any term, covenant, or condition of this Agreement be invalid or unenforceable, the remainder of this Agreement shall not be affected, and the remainder shall be valid and enforceable to the fullest extent permitted by law.

22. This Agreement represents the entire understanding of the Artist and Patron, supersedes any and all other and prior agreements between the Parties, and declares all such prior agreements between the Parties null and void. The terms of this Agreement and all matters relating to it shall be governed by the Uniform Commercial Code and the laws of _____ [list appropriate Country, State, Territory, or Possession].

In witness of their agreement, the Artist and Patron have signed and dated this document below.

Artist _____   Patron _____

Date _____   Date _____

160

Assignment Estimate/Confirmation/Invoice

Client _____   Date_____

Address _____   ❑ Estimate

_____   ❑ Confirmation

Client Purchase Order Number_____   ❑ Invoice

Client Contact _____   Job Number_____

Assignment Description _____

_____

_____

_____

Due Date _____

Grant of Rights. Upon receipt of full payment, Photographer shall grant to the Client the following exclusive rights:

For use as _____

For the product, project, or publication named _____

In the following territory _____

For the following time period or number of uses_____

Other limitations_____

Credit. The Photographer ❑ shall ❑ shall not

receive adjacent credit in the following form on reproduction _____

Fee/Expenses. The Client shall pay the Balance Due, including reimbursement of the expenses as shown below, within thirty days of receipt of an invoice.

Expenses		Fees	
Assistants	$_____	Photography fee	$_____
Casting	$_____	Other fees	
Crews/Special Technicians	$_____	Pre-production $_____/day;	$_____
Equipment Rentals	$_____	Travel $_____/day;	$_____
Film and Processing	$_____	Weather days $_____/day	$_____
Insurance	$_____	Space or Use Rate (if applicable)	$_____
Location	$_____	Cancellation fee	$_____
Messengers	$_____	Reshoot fee	$_____
Models	$_____	Fee subtotal	$_____
Props/Wardrobe	$_____	Plus total expenses	$_____
Sets	$_____	Subtotal	$_____
Shipping	$_____	Sales tax	$_____
Styling	$_____	**Total**	**$_____**
Travel/Transportation	$_____	Less advances	$_____
Telephone	$_____	**Balance due**	**$_____**
Other expenses	$_____		
subtotal	$_____		
(Plus _____% markup)	$_____		
Total expenses	**$_____**		

Photographer_____

Client_____

Company Name

By_____

Authorized Signatory, Title

Subject to All Terms and Conditions Above and on Reverse Side

1. **Payment.** Client shall pay the Photographer within thirty days of the date of Photographer's billing, which shall be dated as of the date of delivery of the Assignment. The Client shall be responsible for and pay any sales tax due. Time is of the essence with respect to payment. Overdue payments shall be subject to interest charges of _____ percent monthly.

2. **Advances.** Prior to Photographer's commencing the Assignment, Client shall pay Photographer the advance shown on the front of this form, which advance shall be applied against the total due.

3. **Reservation of Rights.** Unless specified to the contrary on the front of this form any grant of rights shall be limited to the United States for a period of one year from the date of the invoice and, if the grant is for magazine usage, shall be first North American serial rights only. All rights not expressly granted shall be reserved to the Photographer, including but not limited to all copyrights and ownership rights in photographic materials, which shall include but not be limited to transparencies, negatives, and prints. Client shall not modify directly or indirectly any of the photographic materials, whether by digitized encodations or any other form or process now in existence or which may come into being in the future, without the express, written consent of the Photographer.

4. **Value and Return of Originals.** All photographic materials shall be returned to the Photographer by registered mail or bonded courier (which provides proof of receipt) within thirty days of the Client's completing its use thereof and, in any event, within _____ days of Client's receipt thereof. Time is of the essence with respect to the return of photographic materials. Unless a value is specified for a particular image either on the front of this form or on a Delivery Memo given to the Client by the Photographer, the parties agree that a reasonable value for an original transparency is $1,500. Client agrees to be solely responsible for and act as an insurer with respect to loss, theft, or damage of any image from the time of its shipment by Photographer to Client until the time of return receipt by Photographer.

5. **Additional Usage.** If Client wishes to make any additional uses, Client shall seek permission from the Photographer and pay an additional fee to be agreed upon.

6. **Authorship Credit.** Authorship credit in the name of the Photographer, including copyright notice if specified by the Photographer, shall accompany the photograph(s) when it is reproduced, unless specified to the contrary on the front of this form. If required authorship credit is omitted, the parties agree that liquidated damages for the omission shall be three times the invoiced amount.

7. **Expenses.** If this form is being used as an Estimate, all estimates of expenses may vary by as much as ten (10%) percent in accordance with normal trade practices. In addition, the Photographer may bill the Client in excess of the estimates for any overtime which must be paid by the Photographer to assistants and free-lance staff for a shoot that runs more than eight (8) consecutive hours.

8. **Reshoots.** If Photographer is required by the Client to reshoot the Assignment, Photographer shall charge in full for additional fees and expenses, unless (a) the reshoot is due to Acts or God or is due to an error by a third party, in which case the Client shall only pay additional expenses but no fees; or (b) if the Photographer is paid in full by the Client, including payment for the expense of special contingency insurance, then Client shall not be charged for any expenses covered by such insurance in the event of a reshoot. The Photographer shall be given the first opportunity to perform any reshoot.

9. **Cancellation.** In the event of cancellation by the Client, the Client shall pay all expenses incurred by the Photographer and, in addition, shall pay the full fee unless notice of cancellation was given at least _____ hours prior to the shooting date in which case fifty (50%) percent of the fee shall be paid. For weather delays involving shooting on location, Client shall pay the full fee if Photographer is on location and fifty (50%) percent of the fee if Photographer has not yet left for the location.

10. **Releases.** The Client shall indemnify and hold harmless the Photographer against any and all claims, costs, and expenses, including attorney's fees, due to uses for which no release was requested or uses which exceed the uses allowed pursuant to a release.

11. **Samples.** Client shall provide the Photographer with two copies of any authorized usage.

12. **Assignment.** Neither this Agreement nor any rights or obligations hereunder shall be assigned by either of the parties, except that the Photographer shall have the right to assign monies due hereunder. Both Client and any party on whose behalf Client has entered into this Agreement shall be bound by this Agreement and shall be jointly and severally liable for full performance hereunder, including but not limited to payments of monies due to the Photographer.

13. **Arbitration.** All disputes shall be submitted to binding arbitration before _____ in the following location _____ and settled in accordance with the rules of the American Arbitration Association. Judgment upon the arbitration award may be entered in any court having jurisdiction thereof. Disputes in which the amount at issue is less than $_____ shall not be subject to this arbitration provision.

14. **Miscellany.** The terms and conditions of this Agreement shall be binding upon the parties, their heirs, successors, assigns, and personal representatives; this Agreement constitutes the entire understanding between the parties; its terms can be modified only by an instrument in writing signed by both parties, except that the Client may authorize additional fees and expenses orally; a waiver of a breach of any of its provisions shall not be construed as a continuing waiver of other breaches of the same or other provisions hereof; and the relationship between the Client and Photographer shall be governed by the laws of the State of _____.

CHAPTER 11

DEALING WITH

AGENTS

Many photographers are successful in selling their own work, either directly to clients or to intermediaries such as galleries. Other photographers are employed on a regular basis—for example as staff photographers for newspapers. A third group of photographers are independent and depend on stock agencies to make their work available to the largest possible number of potential buyers. A very small number of photographers—the handful who have reached the top of their profession—employ the services of personal photographic agents to assist in obtaining commissions or in selling existing work.

Stock Agents

Stock agents keep files of photographs classified by subject. Ordinarily, they sell the use of a photograph for one time by the buyer—this arrangement is analogous to a rental. Usually, stock agents keep fifty percent of the proceeds of a sale. For foreign sales where foreign subagents are involved, the typical split is one-third to the foreign subagent, one-third to the photographer's main agency, and one-third to the photographer.

Most agencies will require a signed written agreement before they will deal with you. These agreements can vary greatly. If the agency requires an exclusivity agreement to sell your work, be sure to restrict the contract to the specific geographic areas where the agency is active. The exclusivity may also be limited to certain markets, such as to books or magazines. The contract should state that sales of original works are not within the scope of the agency agreement. You should also take into consideration any plans to sell your work overseas when entering into such an agreement.

There are some agencies that will request exclusivity with respect to the clients to whom they sell your work. This type of an agreement should be entered into only when the agency has a buyer that they sell to on a regular basis. Even so, under those circumstances, if you sell your work directly to the client, the agency should receive a commission more in the neighborhood of twenty-five percent as opposed to the standard fifty percent.

Do not enter into an agreement that gives an agency exclusive rights to all of your future work. You may find that an agency is stronger in certain markets than others, and you do not want to tie yourself to their limitations.

Many photographers prefer to place different copies of their work with more than one stock agent (assuming they have non-exclusive agency agreements). One way a photographer can accomplish the multiple placement is by taking several shots of important subjects. In the past this could also be done by making duplicate slides, but that practice is being discouraged now because of the risk of different agencies selling the one-time use of what is believed to be a unique image and turns out not to be. Enough legal problems have resulted from the use of duplicate slides to cause agencies to advise photographers to shoot slightly different views of important subjects when making use of more than one stock agency—and to avoid making duplicate slides. Some stock agents request that photographers type captions and affix them to the mounts of transparencies and include the letters MRA, which mean Model Release Available. Stock houses have different requirements as to film, paper, and size of transparencies.

Your agreement with the agency should require the agency to use best efforts to sell your work and to promptly inform you with respect to all negotiations and other matters involving your work. You will also want the agreement to state that a contract negotiated by the agency is not binding unless it is signed by you.

The agreement also should give you the right to accept or reject any assignment obtained by the agency, and require the agency to keep confidential all matters handled by the agency for you.

The samples you will provide the agency also should be specified in the agreement, and if the samples are valuable, their value should be included.

Stock agencies are responsible for works while they are in the agency's possession, but to better protect yourself, have the contract raise the agent's responsibilities for samples to strict liability (i.e., the agency will be liable whether or not it is at fault) for loss or damage. It is because of their responsibility for works that most stock agencies require individuals who remove transparencies from the agencies to sign for them. In one case, an advertising agency was held liable for $94,500 plus costs and attorney's fees when it lost sixty-three transparencies that it had borrowed. The stock agency, National Stock Network, used an ASMP form which contained a provision stating that the parties agreed that the value of each transparency would be $1,500. The form also required all disputes to be submitted to binding arbitration. For this reason, the proceeding was resolved more expeditiously than it would have been if it had been handled in the traditional manner by a judge and jury.

Most agencies will require a certain period of time after the contract expires to locate and return your materials. You should request a shorter period if you feel the time specified by the agency is too long. Your contract should also clearly state that you are the owner of the material and that the agency is holding it for consignment purposes only. Some states have special artist/gallery consignment laws which might cover you as a photographer. If your state does not have such a law, or the statute does not cover your situation, then you must file a form known as an "UCC 1" with the appropriate officials, usually the Secretary of State, and perhaps the County Clerk. This will help prevent a delay in the return of your material should the agency dissolve or go into bankruptcy. If the agency is sold, or your specific agent leaves the agency, there also should be a provision in your agreement that allows you the option to sever the relationship if you so desire.

The term of the arrangement should be spelled out and provision made for termination under certain circumstances. You should, for example, be permitted to terminate for certain abuses such as failure to pay in a timely fashion or refusing to provide your work when requested. If the contract is for a relatively long period, you should include a clause allowing you to terminate if the agent fails to generate a certain level of sales.

Be careful not to overlook a renewal clause in your contract. Some agencies will want to set up provisions calling for automatic renewal for an additional three or five years unless you notify the agency by a specific date. Try to avoid signing such an agreement. It is a great deal

165

easier to simply renew a contract that you are comfortable with, than to try and get out of a contract that was renewed because you forgot to send the notice in by the specified date. The contract also should specify what is to happen with regard to the agent's commission if the relationship is terminated. Will the agent be entitled to commissions for a certain period after termination, or will the agent receive a fixed sum as compensation? You should also be sure the contract contains a clause reserving any rights not granted to the agent.

For information on how to locate a stock agent in your area, contact Photographers Agency Counsel of America (PACA), P.O. Box 308, Northfield, MN 55057.

The Personal Agent

The *personal photographic agent* usually handles all the work of a few clients. The agent knows buyers and usually makes the initial contact with them on behalf of the photographer. The agent may obtain assignments and do billing and promotion and may act as a business manager and marketer. One way to find a personal photographic agent is to write to SPAR (Society of Photographer and Artist Representatives), 60 East 42nd Street, Suite 1166, New York, NY 10165. SPAR sells a list that outlines its members' specialties and clients. Photographic representatives usually charge a twenty-five percent commission.

Most contracts of this sort provide for a thirty-day notice of termination by either party. Generally, however, the representative will receive a certain commission for work obtained during a period of time (usually not more than six months) after the agreement is terminated. The rep will, of course, be entitled to payment for all work acquired prior to termination regardless of when payment is received. When a photographer has existing accounts, known as *house accounts*, their disposition should be discussed. Will the photographer continue to work for them and not be required to pay an agent commission for this work? Will the house accounts become part of the arrangement to be serviced by the agent for a reduced commission or standard fees? All of these possibilities can be worked out and should be negotiated when the relationship between the photographer and agent begins.

A personal photographic agent performs a wide variety of services, but when acting as matchmaker between a photographer and a client, the agent must be sensitive to the needs of both parties. If those needs are in conflict, the agent will have to act as a negotiator. This intermediary role is never more important than in contractual matters.

If a client is interested in commissioning a work, the process of negotiating a photographer-client contract begins. The institutional client generally may offer the photographer a form or standard contract, but such a contract is rarely accepted in its entirety. Rather, a series of offers and counteroffers will ensue until mutually satisfactory terms have been agreed upon, or until it becomes apparent that an agreement cannot be reached. Non-institutional customers may not have forms; therefore the photographer or agent may have to provide the draft contract.

The agent's role in contract negotiations will normally be to attempt to get the best contract possible for the photographer without unduly antagonizing the customer. Most clients are glad to negotiate with an agent, because agents familiar with the legal and trade terminology and practices tend to facilitate the process. Moreover, since agents are constantly involved in negotiations between various photographers and clients, they are usually in the best position to identify an acceptable contract, and can be trusted to moderate unreasonable or unrealistic demands made by either party.

An *assignment representative* is also an agent and works closely with a photographer. Their job is to continually show and promote your work to prospective clients. This is a relationship that is often exclusive and should be confirmed in writing.

As with a stock agency, the exclusiveness of the contract with your assignment representative should be very specific with respect to the geographic territory and medium the rep is to cover. It is not uncommon to have different reps in different major cities and covering different media such as television and magazines.

The commission rate varies more with an assignment representative than with a stock agency due to the nature of the relationship with a rep. One rep may be representing you to major television networks, while another is handling your local advertising. Depending on the geographic area the agent is covering, and the targeted clients, the commission rate can vary from five to seven percent of gross billing of a television commercial to twenty-five percent of the fee you charged the client. Reps specializing in photojournalism generally have higher rates. Be sure to specify what the commission is and if and under what circumstances it will change.

Usually it is the photographer that handles the billing and pays the rep a commission after the client money is received. This is probably the best arrangement to have as you do not want to be placed in the situation of having already paid your rep before you discover a problem in collecting from your client. If the agent collects the money, you do not want to have to chase the agent down after your client has paid. It has been held that once a client has paid the agent, the obligation is discharged.

Similarly, you should clarify with your rep who will pay for promotional expenses such as advertising. Usually, the cost is split between the rep and the photographer. The amount of the split should initially be determined by you and your rep. If you are splitting costs, there should be some agreement regarding who is to be initially responsible for paying those costs. If the rep is late in paying a bill, for example, you do not want to be personally accountable for any associated late charges.

Suggested Precautions

To protect against possible liability, a photographer should choose an experienced, legitimate agency or agent and clearly delineate the scope of that party's authority in a well-drafted agency agreement checked over by a lawyer familiar with photography law. Most established agencies have their own form contracts, so your attorney should assist you in evaluating the acceptability of the agency's contract. If you will be using the services of a personal photographic agent, you should take care to define the scope of the agent's authority.

ESTATE
PLANNING

Proper estate planning will require the assistance of a knowledgeable lawyer and perhaps also a life insurance agent, an accountant, or a bank trust officer, depending on the nature and size of the estate. In this chapter we will consider the basic principles of estate planning. This discussion is not a substitute for the aid of a lawyer experienced in estate planning; rather, it is intended to introduce you to the basic principles, alert you to potential problems, and aid in preparing you to work with your estate planner(s).

Most fine art photographers, for example, want to have their work preserved. Commercial photographers often have personal work along with the commercial work they hope will continue to generate revenues for their heirs. Even a photographer with modest assets should have an estate plan or will prepared. Apart from the financial and tax planning aspects, it is important to specify what happens to your work after your death.

The Will

A will is a legal instrument by which a person directs the distribution of property in his or her estate upon death. The maker of the will is called the *testator*. Gifts given by a will are referred to as *bequests* (personal property) or *devises* (real estate). Certain formalities are required by state law to create a valid will. About thirty states allow *only* formally witnessed wills; they require that the instrument be in writing and signed by the testator, in the presence of two or more witnesses. The other half of the states allow *either* witnessed or unwitnessed wills. If a will is entirely hand-written and signed by the testator, it is known as a holographic will.

A will is a unique document in two respects. First, if properly drafted it is *ambulatory*, meaning it can accommodate change, such as applying to property acquired after the will is made. Second, a will is *revocable*, meaning that the testator has the power to change or cancel it. Even if a testator makes a valid agreement not to revoke the will, the power to revoke it remains, though liability for breach of contract could result.

Generally, courts do not consider a will to have been revoked unless it can be established that the testator either (1) performed a physical act of revocation, such as burning or tearing up a will, with intent to revoke it; or (2) executed a valid later will which revoked the previous will. Most state statutes also provide for automatic revocation of a will in whole or in part if the testator is subsequently divorced or married.

To modify a will, the testator must execute a supplement, known as a codicil, which has the same formal requirements as those for creating a will. To the extent that the codicil contradicts the will, those contradicted parts of the will are revoked.

Payment of Testator's Debts

When the property owned by the testator at death is insufficient to satisfy all the bequests in the will after all debts and taxes have been paid, some or all of the bequests in the will must be reduced or even eliminated entirely. The process of reducing or eliminating bequests is known as *abatement*, and the priorities for reduction are set according to the category of each bequest. The legally significant categories of gifts are generally as follows: *specific* bequests or devises, meaning gifts of identifiable items ("I give to X all the furniture in my home"); *demonstrative* bequests or devises, meaning gifts which are to be paid out of a specified source unless that source contains insufficient funds, in which case the gifts will be paid out of the general assets ("I give to Y $1,000 to be paid from my shares of stock in ABC Corporation");

170

general bequests, meaning gifts payable out of the general assets of an estate ("I give Z $1,000"); and finally, *residuary* bequests or devises, or gifts of whatever is left in the estate after all other gifts and expenses are satisfied ("I give the rest, residue and remainder of my estate to Z").

Intestate property, or property not governed by a will, is usually the first to be taken to satisfy claims against the estate. (If the will contains a valid residuary clause, there will be no such property.) Next, residuary bequests will be taken. If more money is needed, general bequests will be taken, and lastly, specific and demonstrative bequests will be taken together in proportion to their value. Some states provide that all gifts, regardless of type, abate proportionately.

Disposition of Property Not Willed

If the testator acquires more property during the time between signing the will and death, the disposition of such property will also be governed by the will, which, as we have seen, is ambulatory in nature. If such property falls within the description of an existing category in the will ("I give all my stock to X; I give all my real estate to Y"), it will pass along with all similar property. If it does not, and the will contains a valid residuary clause, such after-acquired property will go to the residuary legatees. If there is no such clause which applies to this property, such property will pass outside the will to the persons specified in the state's law of intestate succession.

When a person dies without leaving a valid will, this is known as dying *intestate*. The property of a person who dies intestate is distributed according to the state law of intestate succession, which specifies who is entitled to what parts of the estate. An intestate's surviving spouse will always receive a share, generally at least one-third of the estate. An intestate's surviving children likewise always get a share. If some of the children do not survive the intestate, the grandchildren of the intestate may be entitled to a share by representation. *Representation* is a legal principle which means that if an heir does not survive the decedent, but has a child who does survive, that child will represent the non-surviving heir and receive that parent's share in the estate. In other words, the surviving child stands in the shoes of a dead parent in order to inherit from a grandparent who dies intestate.

If there are no direct descendants surviving, the intestate's surviving spouse will take the entire estate or share it with the intestate's parents. If there is neither a surviving spouse nor any surviving direct descendant of the intestate, the estate will be distributed to the intestate's parents or, if the parents are not surviving, to the intestate's siblings by representation. If there are no surviving persons in any of these categories, the estate will go to surviving grandparents and their direct descendants. In this way, the family tree is constantly expanded in search of surviving relatives. If none of the persons specified in the law of intestate succession survive the testator, the intestate's property ultimately goes to the state. This is known as *escheat*. It should be noted that the laws of intestate succession make no provision for friends, in-laws, or stepchildren.

State law will often provide a testator's surviving spouse with certain benefits from the estate even if the spouse is left out of the testator's will. Historically, these benefits were known as *dower*, in the case of a surviving wife, or *curtesy*, in the case of a surviving husband. In place of the old dower and curtesy, modern statutes give the surviving spouse the right to "elect" against the will, and thereby receive a share equal to at least one-fourth of the estate. Here again, state laws vary; in some states, the surviving spouse's elective share is one-third. The historical concepts of dower and curtesy are in large part a result of the law's traditional recognition of an absolute duty on the part of the husband to provide for the wife. Modern laws are perhaps better justified by the notion that most property in a marriage should be shared because the financial success of either partner is due to the efforts of both.

Advantages to Having a Will

Now that we have some background as to what a will is and what happens without one, we can begin to look at some of the benefits of having a will.

A will affords the opportunity to direct distribution of one's property and to set out limitations by making gifts conditional. For example, if an individual wishes to donate certain property to a specific charity, but only if certain conditions are adhered to, a will can make such conditions a prerequisite to the donation.

A will permits the testator to nominate an executor, called a "personal representative" in some states, to administer the estate. If no executor is named in the will, the court will appoint one. If the testator has an unusual type of property, such as photography, antiques, art, or publishable manuscripts, it is a good idea to appoint joint executors, one with financial expertise and the other with expertise in valuation of photography, antiques, art, or with publishing. If joint executors are used, some provision should be made in the will for resolving any deadlock between the two. For example, a neutral third party might be appointed as an arbitrator who is directed to resolve any impasses after hearing both sides. It is also advisable to define the scope of the executor's power by detailed instructions. Photographers may wish to appoint a special executor solely for the purpose of dealing with their photography collection. This person, commonly known as a photographic executor, should be experienced in the photography business and you should determine whether he or she will treat your work in a manner which is consistent with your objectives. A lawyer's help will be necessary to set forth all of these important considerations in legally enforceable, unambiguous terms. It is essential in a will to avoid careless language which might be subject to attack by survivors unhappy with the will's provisions. A lawyer's help is also crucial to avoid making bequests which are not legally enforceable because contrary to public policy.

In addition to giving the testator significant posthumous control over division of property, a carefully drafted will can greatly reduce the overall amount of estate tax paid at death. The following information on taxing structures relates to federal estate taxation. State estate taxes often contain similar provisions, but state law must always be consulted for specifics.

The Gross Estate

The first step in evaluating an estate for tax purposes is to determine the so-called "gross estate." The *gross estate* will include all property over which the deceased had significant control at the time of death. Examples would include certain life insurance proceeds and annuities, jointly-held interests, and revocable transfers.

Under current tax laws, the executor of an estate may elect to value the property in the estate either as of the date of death or as of a date six months after death. The estate property must be valued in its entirety at the time chosen. However, if the executor elects to value the estate six months after death and certain pieces of property are distributed or sold before then, that property will be valued as of the date of distribution or sale.

Fair market value is defined as the price at which property would change hands between a willing buyer and a willing seller, when both buyer and seller have reasonable knowledge of all relevant facts. Such a determination is often very difficult to make, especially when items such as artwork or photographs are involved. Although the initial determination of fair market value is generally made by the executor when the estate tax return is filed, the Internal Revenue Service may disagree with the executor's valuation and assign assets a much higher fair market value.

When an executor and the Internal Revenue Service disagree as to valuation, the court will decide the matter. In most cases, the burden will be on the taxpayer to prove the value of the asset. Thus, expert testimony and evidence of the sale of the same or similar properties will be helpful, as in cases involving original manuscripts, drawings, and photographs. In general, courts are reluctant to determine valuation by formula.

Some artists have intentionally destroyed some of their work during their lifetime in order to avoid having those pieces included in their estate for tax purposes. Others have held back work deemed inferior only to have that work displayed after their death. The items which the French government obtained from the Picasso estate were considered extremely bad examples of the late artist's work and were probably warehoused by Picasso because he thought they should be overpainted. Perhaps identification of inferior work by marking or listing in a catalog would be of benefit to the executor.

Generally, estate taxes must be paid when the estate tax return is filed (within nine months of the date of death) although arrangements may be made to spread payments out over a number of years, if necessary. It is not uncommon for executors to be forced to sell properties for less than full value in order to pay taxes. This can be avoided by obtaining insurance policies, the proceeds of which can be set up in a trust. (For an explanation of a trust, see the section "Distributing Property Outside the Will," below.)

The law allows a number of deductions from the gross estate in determining the amount of the taxable estate. The taxable estate is the basis upon which the tax owing is computed. The following section gives you a closer look at some of the key deductions used to arrive at the amount of your taxable estate.

The Taxable Estate

Figuring the taxable estate is the second major step in evaluating an estate for tax purposes, after determining the gross estate. Typical deductions from the gross estate include funeral expenses; certain estate administration expenses; debts and enforceable claims against the estate; mortgages and liens; and, perhaps most significant, the marital deduction and the charitable deduction.

The marital deduction allows the total value of any interest in property which passes from the decedent to the surviving spouse to be subtracted from the value of the gross estate. The government will eventually get its tax on this property, when the spouse dies, but only to the extent such interest is included in the spouse's gross estate. This deduction may occur even in the absence of a will making a gift to the surviving spouse, since state law generally provides that the spouse is entitled to at least one-fourth of the overall estate regardless of the provisions of the will.

The charitable deduction refers to the tax deduction allowed upon the transfer of property from an estate to a recognized charity. Since the definition of a charity for tax purposes is quite technical, it is advisable to insert a clause in the will which provides that if the institution specified to receive the donation does not qualify for the charitable deduction, the bequest shall go to a substitute qualified institution at the choice of the executor.

Once deductions are figured, the taxable estate is taxed at the rate specified by the Unified Estate and Gift Tax Schedule. The unified tax imposes the same rate of tax on gifts made by will as on gifts made during life. It is a progressive tax, meaning the percent paid in taxes increases with the amount of property involved. The rates rise significantly for larger estates, for example, from eighteen percent where the cumulative total of taxable estate and taxable gifts is under $10,000, to fifty-five percent where the cumulative total is over $3,000,000. Tax credits are provided by year according to the tax schedule. Federal estate tax is also reduced by state death tax credit or actual state death tax, whichever is less. Tax credits result in a $600,000 exemption, which is available to every estate. This exemption, combined with the unlimited marital deduction, allows most estates to escape estate taxes altogether.

Distributing Property Outside the Will

Property can be distributed outside of the will by making *inter vivos* gifts (given during the giver's lifetime) either outright or by placing the property in trust prior to death. The main advantage to distributing property outside of the will is that the property escapes the delays and expense of probate, the court procedure by which a will is validated and administered. It used to be that there were also significant tax advantages to making *inter vivos* gifts rather than gifts by will, but since the estate and gift-tax rates are now unified, there are few remaining tax advantages. One remaining advantage to making an *inter vivos* gift is that if the gift appreciates in value between the time the gift is made and death, the appreciated value will not be taxed. If the gift were made by will, the added value would be taxable, since the gift would be valued as of date of death (or six months after). This value difference can represent significant tax savings for the heirs of someone whose practice suddenly becomes successful and rapidly increases in value.

The other advantage to making an *inter vivos* gift involves the yearly exclusion. A yearly exclusion of $10,000 per recipient is available on *inter vivos* gifts. For example, if $15,000 worth of gifts were given to an individual in one year, only $5,000 worth of gifts will actually be taxable to the donor (who is responsible for the gift tax). A married couple can combine their gifts and claim a yearly exclusion of $20,000 per recipient. Gifts made within three years of death used to be included in the gross estate on the theory that they were made in contemplation of death. Recent amendments to the tax laws, however, have done away with the three-year rule for most purposes. The three-year rule is still applicable to gifts of life insurance and to certain transfers involving stock redemptions or tax liens; the rule also applies to certain valuation schemes, the details of which are too complex to discuss here.

Gift-tax returns must be filed by the donor for any year where gifts made exceeded $10,000 to any one donee. It is not necessary to file returns when a gift to any one donee amounts to less than $10,000. However, where it is possible that valuation of the gift will become an issue with the IRS, it may be a good idea to file a return anyway. Filing the return starts the three-year statute of limitations running. Once the statute of limitations period has expired, the IRS will be barred from filing suit for unpaid taxes or for tax deficiencies due to higher government valuations of the gifts. If a taxpayer omits includable gifts amounting to more than twenty-five percent of the total amount of gifts stated in the return, the statute of limitations is extended to six years. There is no statute of limitations for fraudulent returns filed with the intent to evade tax.

In order to qualify as an *inter vivos*, or living, gift for tax purposes, a gift must be complete and final. Control is an important issue. If a giver retains the right to revoke a gift, the gift may be found to be testamentary in nature, even if the right to revoke was never exercised (unless the gift was made in trust). The gift must also be delivered. An actual, physical delivery is best, but a symbolic delivery may suffice if there is strong evidence of intent to make an irrevocable gift. An example of symbolic delivery is when the donor puts something in a safe and gives the intended recipient the only key.

Another common way to transfer property outside the will is to place the property in a trust which is created prior to death. A *trust* is simply a legal arrangement by which one person holds certain property for the benefit of another. The person holding the property is the *trustee*; those for whose benefit it is held are the *beneficiaries*. To create a valid trust, the giver must identify the trust property; make a declaration of intent to create the trust; transfer property to the trust; and name identifiable beneficiaries. If no trustee is named, a court will appoint one. The settlor, or creator of the trust, may also be designated as trustee, in which case segregation of the trust property satisfies the delivery requirement. Trusts can be created by will, in which case they are termed testamentary trusts, but these trust properties will be probated along with the rest of the will. To avoid probate, the settlor must create a valid *inter vivos* trust—one given while the giver is alive.

Generally, in order to qualify as an *inter vivos* trust, a valid interest in property must be transferred before the death of the creator of the trust. If the settlor fails to name a beneficiary for the trust or make delivery of the property to the trustee before death, the trust will likely be termed testamentary. Such a trust will be deemed invalid unless the formalities required for creating a will were complied with.

A trust will not be termed testamentary simply because the settlor retained significant control over the trust, such as the power to revoke or modify the trust. For example, when a person makes a deposit in a savings account in his or her own name as trustee for another, and reserves the power to withdraw the money or revoke the trust, the trust will be enforceable by the beneficiary upon the death of the depositor, providing the depositor has not, in fact, revoked the trust. Many states allow the same type of arrangement in authorizing joint bank accounts with rights of survivorship as valid will substitutes. Property transferred under one of these arrangements is thus passed outside the will and need not go through probate. However, even though such an arrangement escapes probate, the trust property will probably be counted as part of the gross estate for tax purposes because the settlor retained significant control. In addition, if the deceased settlor created a revocable trust for the purpose of decreasing the share of a surviving spouse, in some states the trust will be declared illusory—in effect, invalid. The surviving spouse is then granted the legal share not only from the probated estate but from the revocable trust.

Life insurance trusts can be used for paying estate taxes. The proceeds will not be taxed if the life insurance trust is irrevocable and the beneficiary is someone other than the estate, such as a friend or relative in an individual capacity or the practice. This is especially important, since without a life insurance trust survivors might be forced to sell estate assets for less than their real value in order to pay estate taxes.

Photographers may keep their names "alive" for future generations by selling bodies of work to museums and art galleries. This also serves to reduce the value of their gross estate. Bradley Smith, a photographer who had worked for *Life* magazine for over twenty years, sold his collection of photographs of paintings from all over the world, in order to "dispose of them." However, without international acclaim such as Smith has, it may be more difficult to sell your work in bulk.

Another consideration would be to donate your work to a library, historical society, university, or the like. You can probably get a tax write-off based on the cost of the material, or your heirs could donate it for full value.

You should first discuss your plans with the institution before making any sort of transfer. Find out how your work will be cared for; look into the institution's means of support, the condition of their files, and the quality of prints released from their collections. You should not relinquish your work to any organization until you are confident that they not only want it, but have the funds to properly care for it.

You should also discuss their plans for use of your work and any income that may be derived from it. Who will retain the artistic control and copyright? It could be anyone from the museum to one of your family members or a trusted friend. You could also license the museum or library to use your work for educational purposes only and retain any income generated from the work. If you possess a large, valuable collection of photographs, you may want to set up a foundation—create your own "charity."

Ansel Adams made careful plans for the disposition of his work which included both a charitable organization and a profit-making trust. Adams sold his negatives to the Center for Creative Photography (CCP) for a modest sum. When Adams died in 1984, he left detailed instructions about how his negatives could be used by CCP for educational purposes only. His fine prints and other work he had collected were donated. However, Adams retained the copyrights to exploit his work for the purpose of establishing the Ansel Adams Publishing Rights Trust, which retains control of all publishing, licensing, and reproduction rights. The trustees of this trust also supervise the archives where the negatives are stored.

Profits from the trust are split two ways: part goes to support the archives at the CCP; and part goes to the Ansel Adams family trust which manages the gross estate and personal property.

In all these matters, a famous photographer has the edge. The majority of photographers may have to settle for less favorable arrangements when selling or donating their work.

All professional photographers should give some thought to estate planning and take the time to execute a will. Without a will, there is simply no way to control the disposition of one's property. In addition, you should keep good records. Cataloging your work will aid both during your lifetime and after your death. Whether you dispose of your photography by will or in some other way, it is essential to identify the size of your holdings as well as the copyrights possessed by you at death. Sound estate planning may include transfers outside of the will, since these types of arrangements escape the delays and expenses of probate. Certain types of trusts can be valuable will substitutes, but they may be subject to challenge by a surviving spouse. Since successful estate planning is complex, it is essential to work with a lawyer skilled in this field.

13

HOW TO FIND
A LAWYER

Most photographers expect to seek the advice of a lawyer only occasionally, for counseling on important matters such as potential defamation or invasion of privacy liability. If this is your concept of the attorney's role in your profession, I suggest you re-evaluate it. If you are a serious photographer, you should establish an early relationship with an attorney. An attorney experienced in publishing or art law should be able to give you important information regarding areas of liability exposure unique to your work, such as portrayal of someone in a false light, invasion of privacy, pornography and obscenity, libel, copyright infringement, breach of the photographer-customer contract, etc.

If employees assist you in shooting and developing, you should also have advice on your legal relationship with present and future employees. Ignorance of these issues can lead to inadvertent violation of the rules, which in turn can result in financially devastating lawsuits and even criminal penalties. Each state has its own laws covering certain business practices; thus, state laws must be consulted on many areas in this book. A competent local business attorney is, therefore, your best source of information on many issues which will arise in the running of your business.

What is really behind all the hoopla about "preventive legal counseling"? Are we lawyers simply seeking more work? Admittedly, as business people, lawyers want business. But what you should consider is economic reality: Most legal problems cost more to solve or defend than it would have cost to prevent them in the first place. Litigation is notoriously inefficient and expensive. You do not want to sue or to be sued, if you can help it. The expense is shocking; for instance, it can cost close to one hundred dollars per day simply to use a courtroom for trial. Pretrial procedures run into the thousands of dollars on most cases. The cost of defending a case filed against you is something you have no choice about, unless you choose to default, which is almost never advisable.

The lawyer who will be most valuable to you will likely not be a Raymond Burr or Robert Redford character, but rather a meticulous person who does most of his or her work in an office, going over your business forms, your employee contracts, or your corporate bylaws. This person should have a good reputation in the legal community as well as in the business community. You might pay over $150 per hour for the attorney, but if the firm has a good reputation it likely employs a well-trained professional staff that can reduce the amount of attorney time required.

One of the first items you should discuss with your lawyer is the fee structure. You are entitled to an estimate, though unless you enter into an agreement to the contrary with the attorney, the estimate is just that. Business and publishing lawyers generally charge by the hour, though you may be quoted a flat rate for a specific service such as incorporation or review of a contract.

If you do not know any attorneys, ask other photographers and publishers whether they know any good ones. You want a lawyer who specializes in copyright and/or photography law. Finding the lawyer who is right for you is like finding the right doctor; you may have to shop around a bit. Your city, county, and state bar associations may have helpful referral services. A good tip is to find out who is in the intellectual property section of the state or county bar association, or who has served on special bar committees dealing with intellectual property law. (Also contact ASMP for their lawyer referral service.) It may also be useful to find out whether any articles covering the area of law you are concerned with have been published in either scholarly journals or continuing legal-education publications, and if the author is available to assist you. Your state or county law librarian can assist you here.

It is a good idea to hire a specialist, or law firm with a number of specialists, rather than a general practitioner. While it is true that you may pay more per hour for the expert, you will not have to fund his learning time, and experience is valuable. In this regard, you may wish to keep in mind that it is uncommon for a lawyer to specialize in business practice and also handle criminal matters. Thus if you are faced with a criminal prosecution for drunk driving, you should be searching for an experienced criminal defense lawyer.

One method by which you can attempt to evaluate an attorney in regard to representing business clients is by consulting the *Martindale-Hubbell Law Directory* in your local county law library. While this may be useful, the mere fact that an attorney's name does not appear in the book should not be given too much weight, since there is a charge for being included, and some lawyers may have chosen not to pay for the listing.

After you have obtained some names, it would be appropriate for you to talk with several attorneys for a short period of time to evaluate them. Do not be afraid to ask about their background and experience, and whether they feel they can help you.

Once you have completed the interview process, select the lawyer with whom you are most comfortable. The rest is up to you. Contact your attorney whenever you believe you have a legal question.

I encourage my clients to feel comfortable about calling me at the office during the day or at home in the evening. Some lawyers, however, may resent having their personal time invaded. Some, in fact, do not list their home telephone numbers. Learn your attorney's preference early on.

The attorney-client relationship is such that you should feel comfortable when confiding in your attorney. This person will not disclose your confidential communications; in fact, a violation of this rule, depending on the circumstances, can be considered an ethical breach that could subject the attorney to professional sanctions.

If you take the time to develop a good working relationship with your attorney, it may well prove to be one of your more valuable business assets.

For a list of volunteer lawyers organizations, see Appendix III.

ASMP CODE
OF ETHICS

guide for ethical business dealings, protecting the profession, the photographer, vendors, employees, subjects, clients, and colleagues.

Responsibility to colleagues and the profession:

1. Maintain a high quality of service and a reputation for honesty and fairness.
2. Oppose censorship and protect the copyrights and moral rights of other creators.
3. Never advance one's own interests at the expense of the profession.
4. Foster fair competition based on professional qualification and merit.
5. Never deliberately exaggerate one's qualifications, nor misrepresent the authorship of work presented in self-promotion.

6. Never engage in malicious or deliberately inaccurate criticism of the reputation or work of another photographer.
7. Negotiate licensing agreements that protect the historical balance between usage fees and rights granted.
8. Never offer nor accept bribes, kick-backs, or other unethical inducements.
9. Never conspire with others to fix prices, organize illegal boycotts, nor engage in other unfair competitive practices.
10. Refuse agreements that are unfair to the photographer.
11. Never undertake assignments in competition with others for which payment will be received only if the work is accepted.
12. Never enter commercial competitions in which usage rights are transferred without reasonable fees.
13. Donate time for the betterment of the profession and to advise entry-level photographers.

Responsibility to subjects:
14. Respect the privacy and property rights of one's subjects.
15. Never use deceit in obtaining model or property releases.

Responsibility to clients:
16. Conduct oneself in a professional manner, and represent a client's best interests within the limits of one's professional responsibility.
17. Protect a client's confidential information; assistants should likewise maintain confidentiality of the photographer's proprietary information.
18. Accurately represent to clients the existence of model and property releases for photographs.
19. Stipulate a fair and reasonable value for lost or damaged photographs.
20. Use written contracts and delivery memos with a client, stock agency, or assignment representative.
21. Consider an original assignment client's interests with regard to allowing subsequent stock use of that work by the client's direct competition, absent an agreement allowing such use.

Responsibility to employees and suppliers:
22. Honor one's legal, financial and ethical obligations toward employees and suppliers.
23. Never take unfair advantage of one's position as employer of models, assistants, employees or contract labor.

Responsibility of the photojournalist:

24. Photograph as honestly as possible, provide accurate captions, and never intentionally distort the truth in news photographs.
25. Never alter the content or meaning of a news photograph and prohibit subsequent alteration.
26. Disclose any alteration or manipulation of content or meaning in editorial feature or illustrative photographs and require the publisher to disclose that distortion or any further alteration.

TABLE OF

CASES

Campbell v. *Acuff Rose Music*, 972 F.2d 1429 (6th Cir. 1992)

Cantrell v. *Forest City Publishing Co.*, 419 U.S.245 (1974)

CCNV v. *Reid*, 490 U.S. 730 (1989)

Chandler v. *Florida*, 449 U.S. 560 (1981)

Colten v. *Jacques Marchais, Inc.*, 61 N.Y.S.2d 269 (1946)

Commissioner v. *Soliman, ___ U.S. ___*, 113 S. Ct. 701 (1993)

Cory v. *Nintendo of America*, 185 A.D.2d 70, 592 N.Y.S.2d 6 (1993)

Cox Broadcasting Corp. v. *Cohn*, 420 U.S. 469 (1975)

Daily Times Democrat v. *Graham*, 276 Ala. 380, 162 SO. 2d 474 (1964)

Douglass v. *Hustler Magazine, Inc.*, 796 F.2d 1128 (7th Cir. 1985)

Estate of Hemingway v. *Random House, Inc.*, 23 N.Y.2d 341 (1968)

Faloona v. *Hustler Magazine, Inc.*, 799 F.2d 1000 (5th Cir. 1986)

Friedan v. *Friedan*, 414 F. Supp. 77 (1976)

Galella v. *Onassis*, 487 F.2d 986 (2d Cir. 1973), 533 F. Supp. 1076 (S.D.N.Y. 1982)

Ginzburg v. *U.S.*, 383 U.S. 463 (1966)

Gomes v. *Fried*, 136 Cal. App. 3d 924 (1984)

Goor v. *Navilio*, 177 Misc. 970, 31 N.Y.S.2d 619 (1941)

Gross v. *Seligman*, 212 F. 930 (2d Cir. 1914)

Hagler v. *Democrat News, Inc.*, 699 S.W.2d 96 (E.D. Mo. 1985)

Hamling v. *United States*, 418 U.S. 87 (1974)

Horgan v. *Macmillan, Inc.*, 789 F.2d 157 (2d Cir. 1986)

Jacobellis v. *Ohio*, 378 U.S. 184 (1964)

Jenkins v. *Georgia*, 418 U.S. 153 (1974)

Kingsley International Pictures Corp. v. *Regents of the University of New York*, 360 U.S. 684 (1959)

Kois v. *Wisconsin*, 408 U.S. 229 (1972)

Lavin v. *New York News, Inc.*, 757 F.2d 1416 (3d Cir. 1985)

Leverton v. *Curtis Publishing Co.*, 192 F.2d 974 (3d Cir. 1971)

Manual Enterprises v. *Day*, 370 U.S. 478 (1962)

Marco v. *Accent Publishing Co.*, 969 F.2d 1547 (3d Cir. 1992)

Martin Luther King, Jr. Center for Social Change v. *American Heritage*, 694 F.2d 674 (11th Cir. 1983)

Melvin v. *Reid*, 112 Cal. App. 285 (1931)

Memoirs v. *Massachusetts*, 383 U.S. 413 (1966)

Mieske v. *Bartell Drug Co.*, 92 Wash. 2d 40, 593 P.2d 1308 (1979)

Miller v. *California*, 413 U.S. 15 (1973)

Namath v. *Sports Illustrated*, 39 N.Y.2d 897, 352 N.E.2d 584, 386 N.Y.S. 2d 397 (1976)

Near v. *Minnesota*, 283 U.S. 697 (1931)

Nebraska Press Association v. *Stuart*, 427 U.S. 539 (1976)

New York Times v. *Sullivan*, 376 U.S. 254 (1964)

New York Times Co. v. *United States*, 403 U.S. 713 (1971)

New York v. *Ferber*, 458 U.S. 747 (1982)

New York World's Fair 1964-64 Corp. v. *Colourpicture Pub. Inc.*, 21
A.D.2d 896, 251 N.Y.S.2d 885 (1964)

Penthouse Enter. Ltd. v. *Eastman Kodak Co.*, 184 N.J. Super. 130, 445 A.2d
428 (1982)

People v. *Keough*, 31 N.Y.2d 281, 290 N.E.2d 819, 338 N.Y.S.2d 618
(1972)

People v. *Von Rosen*, 13 Ill. 2d 68, 147 N.E.2d 327 (1958)

Peregrine v. *Lauren Corp.*, 601 F. Supp. 828 (Colo. 1985)

Philadelphia Newspapers, Inc. v. *Hepps*, 475 U.S. 767 (1986)

Regina v. *Hicklin*, L.R. 3 Q.B. 360 (1868)

Rinaldi v. *Village Voice, Inc.*, 47 A.D.2d 180 (1975)

Rogers v. *Koons*, 960 F.2d 301 (2d Cir. 1992)

Roth v. *United States*, 354 U.S. 476 (1957)

Rowan v. *United States Post Office Dept.*, 397 U.S. 728 (1970)

Russell v. *Marboro Books*, 18 Misc. 2d 166, 183 N.Y.S.2d 8 (1959)

Sharon v. *Time, Inc.*, 609 F. Supp. 1291 (S.D.N.Y. 1984)

Sherrill v. *Knight*, 569 F.2d 124 (1977)

Shields v. *Gross*, 563 F. Supp. 1253 (S.D.N.Y. 1983)

Sony Corporation of America v. *Universal City Studios, Inc. et al.*, 464
U.S. 417 (1984)

Spahn v. *Julian Messner, Inc.*, N.Y.2d 124, 233 N.E.2d 840 (1967)

Stahl v. *Oklahoma*, 665 P.2d 839 (1983)

Time, Inc. v. *Bernard Geis Associates*, 293 F. Supp. 130 (S.D.N.Y. 1968)

Time, Inc. v. *Hill*, 385 U.S. 347 (1967)

Time, Inc. v. *Firestone*, 424 U.S. 448 (1976)

Time, Inc. v. *Ragano*, 427 F.2d 219 (5th Cir. 1970)

Triangle Publications, Inc. v. *Chumley*, 253 Ga. 179, 317 S.E.2d 534
(1984)

United States v. *The Progressive, Inc.*, 486 F. Supp. 5 (Wisc. 1979)

Virginia State Board of Pharmacy v. *Virginia Consumer Council*, 425 U.S.
748 (1976)

Walt Disney Productions v. *Air Pirates*, 581 F.2d 751 (9th Cir. 1978)

Westmoreland v. *CBS*, 770 F.2d 1168 (D.C. 1985)

White Studio, Inc. v. *Dreyfoos*, 156 A.D. 762, 142 N.Y.S. 37 (1913)

Willard Van Dyke Productions v. *Eastman Kodak*, 12 N.Y.2d 301, 189
N.E.2d 693, 239 N.Y.S.2d 337 (1963)

Young v. *United States*, 71-2 Tax Cas. (CCH) P9643 (1971)

ORGANIZATIONS

THAT OFFER

HELP

Always, your best source for finding the professional who can help you is a friend whose needs have been the same as yours. Chapter 13 offers suggestions for ways of finding a lawyer; in addition to those sources, consider asking the photography or art department of your local college or university for the names of people or groups who might be of help.

The following are some of the best-known and largest of the photographer's organizations and other organizations that can be of help to photographers.

Photographer's Groups

Advertising Photographers of New York
27 West 20th Sreet
New York, NY 10010

American Society of Media Photographers
14 Washington Road, Suite 502
Princeton Junction, NJ 08550-1033

International Photographers Association
111 West Jackson, Suite 1060
Chicago, IL 60604

International Photographers of Motion Picture
    and Television Industries, Local 644
505 8th Avenue, 16th Floor
New York, NY 10018

National Press Photographers Association
3200 Croasdaile Drive, Suite 306
Durham, NC 27705

New York Press Photographers Association
225 East 36th Street
New York, NY 10016

Professional Photographers of America, Inc.
57 Forsythe Street, NW, Suite 1600
Atlanta, GA 30303

Wedding Photographers International
1312 Lincoln Boulevard
Santa Monica, CA 9040

White House News Photographers Association
7119 Ben Franklin Station
Washington, D.C. 20044

Industry Groups

American Society of Picture Professionals
P.O. Box 24201
Nashville, TN 37202

Association of Professional Color Laboratories
603 Lansing Avenue
Jackson, MI 49202

National Association of Photographic Manufacturers
550 Mamaroneck Avenue
Harrison, NY 10528

Picture Agency Council of America (PACA)
Lonnie Tuttle Schroeder, Executive Administrator
P.O. Box 308
Northfield, MN 55057

Society of Motion Picture and Television Engineers
595 West Hartsdale Avenue
White Plains, NY 10607

Society of Photographer and Artist Representatives, Inc.
60 East 42nd Street, Suite 1166
New York, NY 10165

Insurance

Taylor and Taylor Associates,Inc.
205 East 42nd Street
New York, NY 10017

Health and Safety

Arts, Crafts and Theater Safety
181 Thompson Street, # 23
New York, NY 10012

National Institute of Occupational Safety & Health
4676 Columbia Parkway
Cincinnati, OH 45226

Occupational Safety and Health Administration
U.S. Department of Labor
200 Constitution Avenue, NW, Room N3101
Washington, D.C. 20201

Government Agencies

National Center for State Courts
300 Newport Avenue
Williamsburg, VA 23187-8798

Small Business Administration
Washington, D.C. 20416

United States Copyright Office
Library of Congress
Washington, D.C. 20559

Volunteer Lawyer Organizations

California
California Lawyers for the Arts (CLA)
Fort Mason Center
Building C, Room 255
San Francisco, California 94123
(415) 775-7200

California Lawyers for the Arts (CLA)
1549 Eleventh Street, Suite 200
Santa Monica, California 90401
(310) 395-8893

San Diego Lawyers for the Arts
Attention: Peter Karlen
1205 Prospect Street, Suite 400
La Jolla, California 92037
(619) 454-9696

Colorado
Colorado Lawyers for the Arts (COLA)
208 Grant Street
Denver, Colorado 80203
(303) 722-7994

Connecticut
Connecticut Commission on the Arts (CTVLA)
227 Lawrence Street
Hartford, Connecticut 06106
(203) 566-4770

District of Columbia
Washington Volunteer Lawyers for the Arts
Attention: Joshua Kaufman
918 Sixteenth Street, N.W., Suite 503
Washington, D.C. 20006
(202) 429-0229

Washington Area Lawyers for the Arts (WALA)
1325 G Street, NW - Lower Level
Washington, D.C. 20005
(202) 393-2826

Florida
Volunteer Lawyers for the Arts/Broward
   and Business Volunteer Lawyers for the Arts/Broward, Inc.
5900 North Andrews Avenue, Suite 907
Fort Lauderdale, Florida 33309
(305) 771-4131

Business Volunteers for the Arts/Miami (BVA)
150 West Flagler Street, Suite 2500
Miami, Florida 33130
(305) 789-3590

Georgia
Georgia Volunteer Lawyers for the Arts (GVLA)
141 Pryor Street SW, Suite 2030
Atlanta, Georgia 30303
(404) 525-6046

Illinois
Lawyers for the Creative Arts (LCA)
213 West Institute Place, Suite 411
Chicago, Illinois 60610
(312) 944-2787

Kansas
Kansas Association of Non-profits
c/o Susan J. Whitfield-Lungren, Esq.
400 North Woodlawn
East Building, Suite 212
Post Office Box 780227
Wichita, Kansas 67278-0227
(316) 685-3790

Louisiana

Louisiana Volunteer Lawyers for the Arts (LVLA)
c/o Arts Council of New Orleans
821 Gravier Street, Suite 600
New Orleans, Louisiana 70112
(504) 523-1465

Maryland

Maryland Lawyers for the Arts
Belvedere Hotel
1 East Chase Street, Suite 1118
Baltimore, Maryland 21202-2526
(410) 752-1633

Massachusetts

Lawyers for the Arts
The Artists Foundation, Inc.
8 Park Plaza
Boston, Massachusetts 02116
(617) 227-2787

Minnesota

Resources and Counseling, United Arts
429 Landmark Center
75 West 5th Street
St. Paul, Minnesota 55102
(612) 292-3206

Missouri

St. Louis Volunteer Lawyers and Accountants for the Arts (SLVLAA)
3540 Washington
St. Louis, Missouri 63103
(314) 652-2410

Kansas City Attorneys for the Arts
c/o Rosalee M. McNamara
Gage & Tucker
2345 Grand Avenue
Kansas City, Missouri 64108
(816) 474-6460

Montana

Montana Volunteer Lawyers for the Arts
c/o Jean Jonkel, Esq.
P.O. Box 8687

Missoula, Montana 59807
(406) 721-1835

Nevada
Mark G. Tratos
Quirk & Tratos
550 East Charleston Blvd.
Las Vegas, Nevada 89104
(702) 386-1778

New Jersey
New Jersey Bar Committee on Entertainment and The Arts
c/o Mathews, Woodbridge & Collins
Attention: Christopher Sidoti
100 Thanet Circle, Suite 306
Princeton, New Jersey 08540-3662
(609) 924-3773

New York
Volunteer Lawyers for the Arts Program
Albany/ Schenectady League of Arts (ALA)
19 Clinton Avenue
Albany, New York 12207
(518) 449-5380

Volunteer Lawyers for the Arts (VLA)
One East 53rd Street, Sixth Floor
New York, New York 10022
(212) 319-2787

Arts Council in Buffalo and Erie County
c/o Karen Kosman, Program Coordinator
700 Main Street
Buffalo, New York 64141
(716) 856-7520

North Carolina
North Carolina Volunteer Lawyers for the Arts (NCVA)
c/o William F. Moore, Esquire
P.O. Box 26513
Raleigh, North Carolina 27611-6513
(919) 832-9661

Ohio

Volunteer Lawyers and Accountants for the Arts (VLAA)
c/o The Cleveland Bar Association
113 Saint Clair Avenue, Suite 225
Cleveland, Ohio 44114-1253
(216) 696-3525

Toledo Volunteer Lawyers for the Arts
c/o Arnold Gottlieb
608 Madison Avenue
Toledo, Ohio 43604
(419) 255-3344

Oklahoma

Oklahoma Volunteer Lawyers and Accountants for the Arts
Post Office Box 266
Edmond, Oklahoma 73083
(405) 340-7988

Pennsylvania

Philadelphia Volunteer Lawyers for the Arts (PVLA)
The Arts Alliance Building
251 South 18th Street
Philadelphia, Pennsylvania 19103
(215) 545-3385

Rhode Island

Ocean State Lawyers for the Arts (OSLA)
P.O. Box 19
Saunderstown, Rhode Island 02874
(401) 789-5686

Tennessee

Tennessee Arts Commission
Bennett Tarleton
320 Sixth Avenue N.
Nashville, Tennessee 37243-0780
(615) 741-1701

Texas

Austin Lawyers and Accountants for the Arts (ALAA)
340 Executive Center Drive
Austin, Texas 78731
(512) 338-4458

Texas Accountants and Lawyers for the Arts/Dallas
c/o Katherine Wagner
2917 Swiss Avenue
Dallas, Texas 75204
(214) 821-2522

Texas Accountants and Lawyers for the Arts (TALA)
1540 Sul Ross
Houston, Texas 77006
(713) 526-4876

Utah
Utah Lawyers for the Arts (ULA)
170 South Main Street, Suite 1500
Post Office Box 45444
Salt Lake City, Utah 84145-0444
(801) 521-3200

Washington
Washington Lawyers for the Arts (WLA)
219 First Avenue S., Suite 315-A
Seattle, Washington 98104
(206) 292-9171

Australia
Art Law Centre of Australia
Attention: Michael McMahon
The Gunnery
43 Cowper Wharf Road
Woolloomooloo, New South Wales 2011
02-356-2566

Canada
Canadian Artists' Representation Ontario (CARO)
Artist's Legal Advice Services (ALAS - Ontario)
183 Bathurst St., 1st Floor
Toronto, Ontario M5T 2R7, Canada
(416) 360-0780

Canadian Artists' Representation Ontario (CARO)
Artist's Legal Advice Services (ALAS - Ottawa)
189 Laurier Avenue E.
Ottawa, Ontario K1N 6P1, Canada
(613) 235-6277

Canadian Artists' Representation Saskatchewan (CARFAC)
Artist's Legal Advice Services (ALAS - Saskatchewan)
210-1808 Smith Street
Regina, Saskatchewan S4P 2N3, Canada
(306) 522-9788

Puerto Rico
Voluntarios Por Las Artes/Volunteers for the Arts
563 Trigo Street
El Dorado Blvd., Suite 5-B
Miramar, Puerto Rico 00907
(809) 724-0700

BOOKS AND

RESOURCES

C lark, Nancy; Cutler, Thomas; and McGrane, Jean-Ann. *Ventilation: A Practical Guide*. New York: Center for Occupational Hazards, 1980.

Crawford, Tad. *Business and Legal Forms for Photographers*. New York: Allworth Press, 1991.

Crawford, Tad. *Legal Guide for the Visual Artist, 3d ed*. New York: Allworth Press, 1995.

DuBoff, Leonard D. *Art Law in a Nutshell, 2d ed*. St. Paul: West Publishing Co., 1993.

DuBoff, Leonard D. *Business Forms and Contracts (in Plain English)® for Craftspeople, 2d ed*. Loveland, Colorado: Interweave Press, 1993.

DuBoff, Leonard D., and Caplan, Sally Holt. *The Desk Book of Art Law, 2d ed.* Dobbs Ferry, New York: Oceana Press.

DuBoff, Leonard D. *The Law (in Plain English)® for Small Businesses.* New York: Wiley & Sons, 1991.

DuBoff, Leonard, D. *The Photographer's Business and Legal Handbook.* New York: Images Press, 1989.

Gordon, Barbara and Elliott. *How to Sell Your Photographs and Illustrations.* New York: Allworth Press, 1990.

Heron, Michal. *The Photographer's Organizer.* New York: Allworth Press, 1992.

Heron, Michal, and MacTavish, David. *Pricing Photography: The Complete Guide to Assignment and Stock Prices.* New York: Allworth Press, 1993.

Heron, Michal. *Stock Photo Forms.* New York: Allworth Press, 1991.

Leland, Caryn R. *Licensing Art & Design. 2d ed.* New York: Allworth Press, 1995.

Nelson, Norbert. *Photographing Your Product.* New York: Van Nostrand-Reinhold Co., 1971.

Piscopo, Maria. *The Photographer's Guide to Marketing and Self-Promotion.* New York: Allworth Press, 1995.

Schilling, Dana. *Be Your Own Boss: The Complete, Indispensible, Hands-on Guide to Starting and Running Your Own Business.* New York: Penguin Books, 1984.

Schmid, Claus-Peter. *Photography for Artists and Craftsmen.* New York: Van Nostrand-Reinhold Co., 1975.

Shaw, Susan D., and Rossol, Monona. *Overexposure: Health Hazards in Photography. 2d ed.* New York: Allworth Press, 1991.

Government Pamphlets

Internal Revenue Service, *Tax Guide for Small Business*, Publication 334.
National Endowment for the Arts, *Guide to The NEA*, Visual Arts Fellowship Program.

National Endowment for the Arts, *Visual Arts Fellowships*, Visual Arts Fellowship Program.

Small Business Administration, *Insurance and Risk Management for Small Business*, Small Business Management Series No. 30, 2d ed.

Small Business Administration, *Insurance Checklist for Small Business*, Small Marketer's Aid No. 148.

Small Business Administration, *Sound Cash Management and Borrowing*, Publication FM9.

U.S. Department of Labor, *Fire Safety Fact Sheet*, Publications 91-41 and 3088, OSHA Information.

INDEX

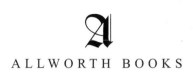

ALLWORTH BOOKS

Allworth Press publishes quality books to help individuals and small businesses. Titles include:

Legal Guide for the Visual Artist, Third Edition
by Tad Crawford (softcover, 8½ × 11, 256 pages, $19.95)

Business and Legal Forms for Photographers
by Tad Crawford (softcover, 8½ × 11, 192 pages, $18.95)

Pricing Photography
by Michal Heron and David MacTavish (softcover, 11 × 8½, 128 pages, $19.95)

Licensing Art & Design, Revised Edition
by Cayrn R. Leland (softcover, 6 × 9, 128 pages, $16.95)

Electronic Design and Publishing: Business Practices
by Liane Sebastian (softcover, 6 × 9, 200 pages, $19.95)

The Photographer's Guide to Marketing and Self-Promotion
by Maria Piscopo (softcover, 6¾ × 10, 176 pages, $18.95)

Mastering Black-and-White Photography
by Bernhard J Suess (softcover, 6¾ × 10, 240 pages, $18.95)

Nature and Wildlife Photography: A Practical Guide to How to Shoot and Sell
by Susan McCartney (softcover, 6¾ × 10, 256 pages, $18.95)

Travel Photography: A Complete Guide to How to Shoot and Sell
by Susan McCartney (softcover, 6¾ × 10, 348 pages, $22.95)

Wedding Photography and Video
by Chuck Delaney (softcover, 6 × 9, 144 pages, $10.95)

Overexposure: Health Hazards in Photography
by Susan D. Shaw and Monona Rossol (softcover, 6¾ × 10, 320 pages, $18.95)

How to Shoot Stock Photos that Sell
by Michal Heron (softcover, 8 × 10, 192 pages, $16.95)

Stock Photo Forms
by Michal Heron (softcover, 8¾ × 11, 32 pages, $8.95)

The Photographer's Organizer
by Michal Heron (softcover, 8½ × 11, 32 pages, $8.95)

How to Sell Photographs and Illustrations
by Elliott and Barbara Gordon (softcover, 8 × 10, 128 pages, $16.95)

The Photographer's Assistant
by John Kieffer (softcover, 6¾ × 10, 208 pages, $16.95)

Please write to request our free catalog. If you wish to order a book, send your check or money order to Allworth Press, 10 East 23rd Street, Suite 400, New York, NY 10010. Include $5 for shipping and handling for the first book ordered and $1 for each additional book. Ten dollars plus $1 for each additional book if ordering from Canada. New York State residents must add sales tax.